TRIUMPHANT

in

Tough Times

NEIL T. ANDERSON

HARVEST HOUSE PUBLISHERS
EUGENE, OREGON

Triumphant in Tough Times
Copyright © 2019 by Neil T. Anderson and Harvest House Publishers
Published by Harvest House Publishers
Eugene, Oregon 97408
www.harvesthousepublishers.com

ISBN 978-0-7369-8800-1 (pbk)
ISBN 978-0-7369-8801-8 (eBook)

Library of Congress Control Number: 2023934165

Who Am I?

*When I look at your heavens, the work of your fingers, the moon
and the stars, which you have set in place, what is man that you
are mindful of him, and the son of man that you care for him?*
PSALM 8:3-4 ESV

"What is man?" is an ontological question concerning the nature of "being." Five centuries before Christ, Thales of Miletus was asked, "What is the most difficult?" He replied, "To know thyself." Twenty-five centuries later, science is no closer to answering "What is man?" We know far more about the chemical makeup of the body, but that tells us nothing about who we are when absent from the body and present with the Lord. Psychology can describe but cannot unlock the mystery of the *person*. Being a carpenter, engineer, parent, or American citizen defines only what we do and where we live, not who we are. Biology is the study of plants and animals, but none bear the image nor likeness of God. Science cannot answer the most basic of all questions: Who are we, and why are we here?

However, Scripture can: "Then the LORD God formed man of dust from the ground, and breathed into his nostrils the breath of life; and man became a living being" (Genesis 2:7 NASB1995). When this happened, something new and totally different was introduced into the universe. God shared His divine and eternal life with Adam, who was created in His image and likeness.

The only "ology" that can properly explain who we are is theology. We are children of Almighty God, created in His image and likeness. Under God's guidance and enabling presence, we are working out our God-given destiny. "We are his workmanship, created in Christ Jesus for good works, which God prepared beforehand, that we should walk in them" (Ephesians 2:10 ESV).

The Holy Spirit's Guidance

For all who are being led by the Spirit of God,
these are sons of God.
ROMANS 8:14

A young pilot had just passed the point of no return when the weather changed for the worse. Visibility dropped to a matter of feet as fog descended to the earth. Putting total trust in the cockpit instruments was a new experience to him, for the ink was still wet on the certificate verifying that he was qualified for instrument flying.

The landing worried him the most. His destination was a crowded metropolitan airport he wasn't familiar with. In a few minutes he would be in radio contact with the tower. Until then, he was alone with his thoughts. His instructor had practically forced him to memorize the rule book. He didn't care for it at the time, but now he was thankful.

Finally he heard the voice of the air traffic controller. "I'm going to put you on a holding pattern," the controller radioed. *Great!* thought the pilot. However, he knew that his safe landing was in the hands of this person. He had to draw upon his previous instructions and training, and trust the voice of an air traffic controller he couldn't see. Aware that this was no time for pride, he informed the controller, "This is not a seasoned pro up here. I would appreciate any help you could give me."

"You've got it!" he heard back.

For the next 45 minutes, the controller gently guided the pilot through the blinding fog. As course and altitude corrections came periodically, the young pilot realized the controller was guiding him around obstacles and away from potential collisions. With the words of the rule book firmly placed in his mind, and with the gentle voice of the controller, he landed safely at last.

The Holy Spirit guides us through the maze of life much like that air traffic controller. The controller assumed that the young pilot understood the instructions of the flight manual. His guidance was based on that. Such is the case with the Holy Spirit: He can guide us if we have a knowledge of God's Word and His will established in our minds.

God Is Holy

*Exalt the L<small>ORD</small> our God, and worship at his holy
mountain; for the L<small>ORD</small> our God is holy!*
P<small>SALM</small> 99:9 <small>ESV</small>

No other attribute in the Bible speaks more directly to God's deity than His holiness. "The Holy One" (Hosea 11:9 <small>ESV</small>) is distinct and separate from all other things. He is "exalted over all the nations" (Psalm 99:2 <small>NIV</small>) and lives above and beyond all creation. The stain of sin and evil that defiled the world never had any effect on God. He has always been morally perfect and separate (or transcendent) from the rest of His fallen creation. "The holy God shows himself holy in righteousness" (Isaiah 5:16 <small>ESV</small>).

The sheer magnitude of God's glory and greatness does not diminish over time. Familiarity does not breed contempt of the Almighty. The holy angels, who have been in His presence since their creation, day and night do not cease to proclaim, "Holy, holy, holy, is the Lord God Almighty, who was and is and is to come!" (Revelation 4:8 <small>ESV</small>).

The prophet Isaiah was given a vision of God seated on a throne. Above the throne were seraphim calling out to one another, "Holy, holy, holy is the L<small>ORD</small> of hosts; the whole earth is full of his glory!" (6:3 <small>ESV</small>). Confronted with God's holiness, Isaiah cried out, "Woe is me! For I am lost; for I am a man of unclean lips, and I dwell in the midst of a people of unclean lips; for my eyes have seen the King, the L<small>ORD</small> of hosts!" (verse 5 <small>ESV</small>). We would all fall on our faces if such a manifestation of God were to come upon us. The only sin we would be aware of is our own. When we distance ourselves from God, we are less aware of our own sins and more aware of other people's sins.

God Is Omnipresent

*If I ascend to heaven, you are there! If I make my bed in
Sheol, you are there! If I take the wings of the morning, and
dwell in the uttermost parts of the sea, even there your hand
shall lead me, and your right hand shall hold me.*
PSALM 139:8-10 ESV

God is everywhere present, even for nonbelievers: "What can be known about God is plain to them, because God has shown it to them. For his invisible attributes, namely, his eternal power and divine nature, have been clearly perceived, ever since the creation of the world, in the things that have been made. So they are without excuse" (Romans 1:19-20 ESV).

God is also present with every believer, but we are only partially present with Him even though our bodies are His temple. We don't always sense His presence because of the daily responsibilities that occupy our minds. It's possible to be so heavenly minded that we are no earthly good. A sinful lifestyle and unresolved conflicts will diminish a sense of His presence. Consciously or subconsciously, we have distanced ourselves from God, but He has not distanced Himself from us. He "will never leave you nor forsake you" (Hebrews 13:5 ESV).

A peaceful sense of His presence comes when we repent and believe again that He is present and live accordingly. This is why we worship God, keeping His divine attributes fresh in our memory. We are the ones who need to consciously keep the divine attributes of God in our minds. He is looking for worshippers who live as though He really is omnipresent. David said, "I have set the LORD always before me; because he is at my right hand, I shall not be shaken" (Psalm 16:8 ESV).

Overcoming the Kingdom of Darkness

The LORD saw that the wickedness of man was great in the earth, and that every intention of the thoughts of his heart was only evil continually. And the LORD regretted that he had made man on the earth, and it grieved him to his heart.

GENESIS 6:5-6 ESV

Adam's sin cost him more than his life. Satan usurped his dominion, and according to Jesus, Satan became "the ruler of this world" (John 14:30 ESV). Satan's rule eventually became so pervasive that God was sorry He created mankind.

That may have been the end of human history if Noah hadn't found grace in the eyes of the Lord. The rebirth of humanity through Noah's family didn't fare much better. God had to deliver His people from slavery in Egypt. The Mosaic covenant promised blessings if they kept the law and punishment if they didn't. The fear of punishment can be a deterrent to sin, but it didn't last. So God sent prophets to call the people to repentance, but they were largely ignored and some even stoned. The kingdom of darkness will rule over those whose "heart is deceitful above all things, and desperately sick" (Jeremiah 17:9 ESV).

Not only are we cursed living under the law (Galatians 3:10), but the law has the capacity to stimulate the desire to do that which it intended to prohibit (Romans 7:5). Tell a child he can't go *there*, and the moment you say it, *there* is where he wants to go. God said Adam could eat from any tree in the Garden of Eden but that one! "Is the law then contrary to the promises of God? Certainly not! For if a law had been given that could give life, then righteousness would indeed be by the law" (Galatians 3:21 ESV).

But God said, "I will give you a new heart, and a new spirit I will put within you" (Ezekiel 36:26 ESV). The New Covenant is grace based. The law is within us, and the sin that separated us from God is forgiven.

Blocked Goals

The fruit of the light consists in all goodness and righteousness and truth.
EPHESIANS 5:9

One morning I rose early, had my devotions, and started making a special breakfast for my family. I was stirring the muffin mix, singing and feeling great, when my sleepy-eyed son, Karl, wandered into the kitchen. He grabbed a box of cereal and an empty bowl and headed for the table.

"Hey, Karl, just a second. We're not having cereal this morning. We're going to sit around the table together and have a big breakfast with muffins."

"I don't like muffins, Dad," he mumbled, opening the cereal box.

"Wait, Karl," I insisted, starting to get annoyed. "We're going to sit around the table together and have a big breakfast with muffins."

"But I don't like muffins, Dad," he repeated.

I lost it. *"Karl, we're going to sit around the table together and have a big breakfast with muffins!"* I barked. Karl closed the cereal box, threw it in the cupboard, and stomped back to his room. My great idea had suddenly turned to shambles. I had to spend the next several minutes apologizing to Karl for my outburst.

Like me, I'm sure you have suffered your share of blocked goals. You had this great plan to do something wonderful for God, your church, your family, or a friend. Then your plan was thrown into disarray by hectic daily events over which you had no control. You didn't get your way at the board meeting. Your child decided to be the lead guitarist in a rock band instead of becoming a doctor like you planned.

When you base your life on the success of plans that are subject to people and circumstances, your life will be one long, emotional roller-coaster ride. And the only way to get off the roller coaster is to walk by faith according to the truth of God's Word. Who you are must not be dependent on the cooperation of others or favorable circumstances. Decide to become the spouse, parent, leader, or worker God wants you to be. No one can block that goal except you.

Successful Christian Living

We are to grow up in all aspects into Him.
EPHESIANS 4:15

It was for freedom that Christ set us free.
GALATIANS 5:1

There are two concepts which determine the victory and fruitfulness of a Christian. The first concept is *maturity*. Paul wrote: "We are to grow up in all aspects into Him, who is the head, even Christ…to a mature man, to the measure of the stature which belongs to the fullness of Christ" (Ephesians 4:15, 13). God has given us everything we need to grow to maturity in Christ (2 Peter 1:3). But Satan is opposed to our maturity and will do anything he can to keep us from realizing who we are and what we have in Christ. We must experience victory over the dark side before we can fully mature.

The second concept of the successful Christian life is *freedom*. Paul declared: "It was for freedom that Christ set us free; therefore keep standing firm and do not be subject again to a yoke of slavery" (Galatians 5:1). This verse not only assures us that God wants us free, but also warns us that we can lose our freedom by returning to the law.

Before we received Christ, we were slaves to sin. But because of Christ's work on the cross, sin's power over us has been broken. Satan has no right of ownership or authority over us. He is a defeated foe, but he is committed to keeping us from realizing that. He knows he can block your effectiveness as a Christian if he can deceive you into believing that you are nothing but a product of your past, subject to sin, prone to failure, and controlled by your habits. As long as he can confuse you and blind you with his dark lies, you won't be able to see that the chains which once bound you are broken. You are free in Christ, but if the devil can deceive you into believing you're not, you won't experience the freedom which is your inheritance. I don't believe in instant maturity, but I do believe in instant freedom, and I have seen thousands of people set free by the truth. Once a person is free, you would be amazed at how quickly he or she matures!

A New Creature

*Therefore if any man is in Christ, he is a new creature; the
old things passed away; behold, new things have come.*
2 CORINTHIANS 5:17

Dan and Cindy were a fine young Christian couple who were preparing for ministry on the mission field. Then tragedy struck: Cindy was raped. As hard as she tried to get back to normal life, Cindy couldn't shake the horrible memories and feelings from her experience.

Six months after the tragedy, Dan and Cindy attended a church conference where I was speaking. During the conference, Cindy called me in tears. "Neil, I know God can turn everything into good, but how is He going to do that?"

"Wait a minute, Cindy," I said. "God will work everything out for good, but He doesn't make a bad thing good. What happened to you was evil. God's good thing is to show you how you can walk through your crisis and come out of it a better person."

"But I just can't separate myself from my experience," she sobbed. "I've been raped, Neil, and I'll be a victim of that all my life."

"No, Cindy," I insisted. "The rape happened to you, but it hasn't changed who you are, nor does it have to control you. You were the victim of a terrible, ugly tragedy. But if you only see yourself as a rape victim for the rest of your life, you will never be free. You're a child of God. You can't fix the past, but you can be free from it."

All of us have a number of hurtful, traumatic experiences in our past which have scarred us emotionally. You may have grown up with a physically, emotionally, or sexually abusive parent. Any number of traumatic, emotional events can clutter your soul with emotional baggage which seems to limit your maturity and block your freedom in Christ. You must renounce the experiences and lies that have controlled you and forgive those who have offended you.

As a Christian, you are primarily the product of the work of Christ on the cross. You are literally a new creature in Christ. The old you is gone; the new you is here.

Union with God

To the saints who are in Ephesus, and are faithful in Christ Jesus:
Grace to you and peace from God our Father and the Lord Jesus Christ.
EPHESIANS 1:1-2 ESV

Paul always identifies Christians as saints, which refers to our identity in Christ and not necessarily to our maturity. The early church understood salvation to mean union with God, and that is most often portrayed by Paul as being "in Christ," or "in Him," or "in the beloved." Forty such prepositional phrases are in the six chapters of Ephesians. God "has blessed us *in Christ*" (Ephesians 1:3 ESV), and He "chose us *in him* before the foundation of the world" (verse 4 ESV). "*In him* we have redemption through his blood, the forgiveness of our trespasses" (verse 7 ESV). "*In him* we have obtained an inheritance" (verse 11 ESV). "*In him* you also, when you heard the word of truth, the gospel of your salvation, and believed *in him*, were sealed with the promised Holy Spirit" (verse 13 ESV). For every verse in the Bible that mentions Christ being in us are ten verses telling us who we are "in Christ."

Before we came to Christ, we were "in Adam," or "in the flesh." We were identified by our natural heritage and sinful nature. Paul, however, never identifies believers by their flesh patterns. We are not sinners; we are saints who sin. Pauline theology is all based on who we are "in Christ." He tells the church in Corinth, "That is why I sent you Timothy, my beloved and faithful child in the Lord, to remind you of my ways *in Christ*, as I teach them everywhere in every church" (1 Corinthians 4:17, ESV). "You, however, are not in the flesh but in the Spirit, if in fact the Spirit of God dwells in you. Anyone who does not have the Spirit of Christ does not belong to him" (Romans 8:9 ESV).

We can't consistently behave in a way that is inconsistent with what we believe about ourselves. What we do doesn't determine who we are; who we are is what determines what we do. So who are we? "Beloved, we are God's children now...and everyone who thus hopes in him purifies himself as he is pure" (1 John 3:2-3 ESV).

Our One Power Source

The surpassing greatness of His power toward us who believe. These
are in accordance with the working of the strength of His might...
EPHESIANS 1:19

In Ephesians 1:19-21, Paul gives us a peek at the dynamic source of our authority in Christ. He explains that the authority at our disposal flows from the reservoir of power which raised Jesus Christ from the dead and seated Him at the Father's right hand. That power source is so dynamic that Paul used four different Greek words in verse 19 to describe it: *power (dunameos), working (energeian), strength (kratous),* and *might (ischuos).* Behind the resurrection of the Lord Jesus Christ lies the mightiest work of power recorded in the Word of God. And the same power which raised Christ from the dead and defeated Satan is the power available to us to overcome the works of Satan in our daily lives.

Paul opens our eyes to the expansive scope of Christ's authority, which is "far above all rule and authority and power and dominion, and every name that is named, not only in this age, but also in the one to come" (Ephesians 1:21). Think about the most powerful and influential political or military leaders in the world. Imagine the most feared terrorists, crime kingpins, and drug barons. Think about the notorious figures of the past and present who have blighted society with their diabolical misdeeds. Think about Satan and all the powers of darkness marshaled under his command. Jesus' authority is not only above all these human and spiritual authorities past, present, and future, but He is *far* above them. We share the same position because we are seated with Christ in the heavenlies, which enables us to live in freedom and victory over demonic intrusion and influence.

Don't be deceived. You are not under Satan's power or subject to his authority. You are in Christ above all demonic rule, authority, and power.

With All Prayer and Petition

With all prayer and petition, pray at all times in the Spirit, and with this
in view, be on the alert with all perseverance and petition for all the saints.
EPHESIANS 6:18

The mother of one of my seminary students was a psychic. She said to him once, "Jim, have you been praying for me?"

"Of course I have, Mother."

"Well, don't," she insisted, "because you're disturbing my aura."

I say pray on! We never know completely the effects of our prayers, but we do know that God includes prayer as part of His strategy for establishing His kingdom and ensuring our spiritual victory.

One of the most dramatic deliverances I have observed happened in a man who was a high priest in the upper echelons of Satanism. Six months after he was set free he gave his testimony in our church. At the close of his testimony I asked him, "Based on your experience on 'the other side,' what is the Christian's greatest strategy against demonic influence?"

"Prayer," he answered forcefully. "And when you pray, mean it. Fervent prayer thwarts Satan's activity like nothing else."

What is prayer? It is communication with God by which we express our dependence on Him. God knows what we need in our battle with the powers of darkness, and He is more ready to meet our needs than we are to ask. But until we express our dependence on Him in prayer, God may not act. In prayer we say, "You are the Lord, not I. You know what's best; I don't. I'm not telling You what to do; I'm asking." Prayer is a means by which God guides and protects His children.

Praying in the Spirit is God's way of helping us pray when we don't know how: "The Spirit also helps our weakness; for we do not know how to pray as we should, but the Spirit Himself intercedes for us" (Romans 8:26). *Helps (sunantilambano)* depicts the Holy Spirit's role of coming alongside us in our condition of human frailty and spiritual vulnerability and bearing us to the other side of spiritual protection and victory.

Our Essential Identity

Then God said, "Let Us make man in Our
image, according to Our likeness."
GENESIS 1:26

Adam was created physically and spiritually alive. He possessed eternal life from his first breath and enjoyed God's abiding presence in the Garden of Eden.

Furthermore, unlike the animal kingdom that operated by divine instinct, Adam was created in the likeness of God with a mind, emotions, and will, giving him the ability to think, feel, and choose. No other created being can make that claim.

After creating Adam, God said, "it is not good for the man to be alone" (Genesis 2:18). So He created a suitable helper for him: Eve. They both enjoyed a sense of belonging to God and each other. Not only that, God gave them a purpose: to "rule over the fish of the sea and over the birds of the sky and over the cattle and over all the earth" (Genesis 1:26). Adam and Eve didn't have to search for significance; they had it in their relationship with God. And because God was present with them, they lived in perpetual safety and security.

Eternal life, identity, purpose, significance, security, and a sense of belonging are all attributes of mankind created in the image of God. Adam and Eve experienced these attributes in full measure, and we were destined to enjoy them too. But when Adam sinned, he died spiritually and forfeited everything God had provided. Being separated from God, Adam's glowing attributes became glaring needs.

As children of Adam born separated from God, we come into the world with these same glaring needs. We wander through life striving to make a name for ourselves, looking for security in temporal things, and searching for significance apart from God. Is it a hopeless quest? No! We are able to fulfill these needs by establishing a personal relationship with God through faith in Jesus Christ. Everything Adam enjoyed in the garden before he sinned is now at our disposal.

Spiritually Alive

And this is the testimony: God has given us eternal life,
and this life is in his Son. He who has the Son has life; he
who does not have the Son of God does not have life.
1 JOHN 5:11-12 NIV

When God breathed life into Adam, he was both physically and spiritually alive. Adam was spiritually alive because his soul was in union with God. We were never designed to be separated from God or to live independently of Him. We were born to be spiritually alive.

For the Christian, to be spiritually alive is to be in union with God. This concept is repeatedly presented in Scripture by the prepositional phrase *in Christ*. Being in Christ is the theme of the New Testament. Like Adam, we were created to be in union with God. But Adam sinned and his union with God, and ours as well, was severed. It is God's eternal plan to bring human creation back to Himself and restore the union He enjoyed with Adam at creation. That restored union with God, which we find in Christ, is the essence of our identity.

When you were born again, your soul was united with God and you came alive spiritually, as alive as Adam was in the garden before he sinned. As the New Testament repeatedly declares, you are now in Christ, and Christ is in you. Since Christ who is in you is eternal, the spiritual life you have received from Him is eternal. You don't have to wait until you die to get eternal life; you possess it right now!

The apostle John wrote, "He who has the Son has the life" (1 John 5:12). He probably remembered Jesus' statement to Martha: "I am the resurrection and the life; he who believes in Me shall live even if he dies, and everyone who lives and believes in Me shall never die" (John 11:25-26). After Jesus said this to Martha, He added, "Do you believe this?" (verse 26).

The Word of God is clear: Because of Jesus, we will continue to live spiritually even after we die physically. Do you believe this?

The Effects of the Fall

*Therefore, just as through one man sin entered into the world, and
death through sin, and so death spread to all men, because all sinned.*
ROMANS 5:12

Unfortunately, the idyllic setting in Eden was shattered. Genesis 3 tells the sad story of Adam and Eve's lost relationship with God through sin. The effects of mankind's fall were immediate and far-reaching, infecting every member of the human race.

What happened to Adam and Eve spiritually because of the Fall? They died. Their union with God was severed and they were separated from God. God had specifically said: "You must not eat from the tree of the knowledge of good and evil, for when you eat of it you will surely die" (Genesis 2:17 NIV). They ate and they died.

Did they die physically? No. The process of physical death was set in motion, but they were alive physically for several hundred more years. They died spiritually; their souls were separated from God. They were banished from God's presence. They were cast out of the Garden of Eden (Genesis 3:23-24).

After Adam, everyone who comes into the world is born physically alive but spiritually dead, separated from God. Paul wrote, "As for you, you were dead in your transgressions and sins, in which you used to live" (Ephesians 2:1 NIV).

How did Jesus remedy this problem? First, He died on the cross to cure the disease that caused us to die: sin. Romans 6:23 begins, "The wages of sin is death." Then He rose from the dead to give us spiritual life. The verse continues, "The free gift of God is eternal life in Christ Jesus our Lord." Jesus Himself said, "I came that they might have life" (John 10:10).

The bad news is that, as a child of Adam, you inherited spiritual death. But the eternally good news is that, as a child of God through faith in Christ, you will live forever because of the life He has provided for you.

16

Secure and Significant

Who is God, but the LORD? And who is a rock, except God?—the
God who equipped me with strength and made my way blameless. He
made my feet like the feet of a deer and set me secure on the heights.
PSALM 18:31-33 ESV

Home invasion security systems. Smoke and fire alarms. Health, dental, and life insurance. Job security. None of those guarantee inner security. Your only real security is your eternal life in Christ. "We have this as a sure and steadfast anchor of the soul, a hope that enters into the inner place behind the curtain, where Jesus has gone as a forerunner on our behalf" (Hebrews 6:19-20 ESV).

Many passages of Scripture speak to our security. You are assured that "God causes all things to work together for good to those who love God" (Romans 8:28). You are free from any condemning charges brought against you (verse 31 and following). You cannot be separated from the love of God (verse 35 and following). You have been established, anointed, and sealed by God, who has given you His Spirit in your hearts as a guarantee (2 Corinthians 1:21-22). "Your life is hidden with Christ in God" (Colossians 3:3 ESV). Your "citizenship is in heaven" (Philippians 3:20 ESV). You are born of God, and the evil one cannot touch you (1 John 5:18). You are secure "in Christ."

And, many passages of Scripture speak to our significance. There is joy in heaven when even one sinner repents (Luke 15:7). No child of God is insignificant. "You did not choose me, but I chose you and appointed you that you should go and bear fruit and that your fruit should abide" (John 15:16 ESV). "Do you not know that you are God's temple and that God's Spirit dwells in you?" (1 Corinthians 3:16 ESV). You are an ambassador for Christ (2 Corinthians 5:20). You are God's coworker (6:1). You are seated with Christ in the heavenlies (Ephesians 2:6). You are God's "workmanship, created in Christ Jesus for good works" (verse 10 ESV). You may approach God with confidence (Ephesians 3:12). You are significant "in Christ."

A Higher Priority

For all who are being led by the Spirit of God, these are sons of God.
ROMANS 8:14

Two significant events in my life brought into clear focus the priority of relationship over achievement. Before being called into the ministry, I worked as an aerospace engineer on the Apollo program. I will never forget the day the lunar lander touched down on the moon. This bold headline dominated the front page of the *Minneapolis Star:* "Neil Armstrong Lands on the Moon." It was an achievement I was proud to be part of.

But the really big news came months earlier on page 7 in the third section: "Heidi Jo Anderson, born to Mr. and Mrs. Neil Anderson, Northwestern Hospital, March 12, 1969." That may not sound like big news to you, but it was to her mother and me. Heidi totally took over my den and captured an entire shelf in the refrigerator. She altered our sleeping pattern and restricted our social calendar. But she was ours to hold, to hug, and to care for.

What does God care about moon-shots? They are deeds to be outdone. Somebody will always come along and do it better, faster, and higher. What God cares about is little people like Heidi Jo Anderson, because they will be with Him forever.

The second significant event in my life was receiving my first doctoral degree. But it turned out to be one of the most anticlimactic days of my life. I heard no applause from heaven, and I don't believe my achievement added so much as an asterisk to my name in the Lamb's Book of Life. I was a child of God before that day, and I was still a child of God afterward.

But what happens in heaven when one sinner repents? Applause! Why? Because a relationship with God is eternal, while earthly achievements last only for time. Have you sacrificed the eternal to gain the temporal? Have you ignored personal and spiritual relationships in your pursuit of human achievements? Relationships must always have a higher priority than temporal achievements.

Seeking God's Face

My heart says of you, "Seek his face!" Your face, LORD, I will seek.
PSALM 27:8 NIV

If the sun is shining in the morning, I'll do it."

"If he's there when I open the door, I'll know he's the one."

"If I pass the class on world missions, I'll be a missionary. If not, I'll be a local pastor."

We all know better than this, but it's amazing how often scenarios just like these pop into our minds. Such propositions are referred to as "laying a fleece" before the Lord or "seeking a sign."

The term *fleece* comes from the account of Gideon. In Judges 6, Gideon is called by God to deliver Israel from the Midianites. Gideon questions whether God is even for Israel (verse 13), and he doubts his own ability (verse 15). So he asks God for a sign (verse 17). God gives him one, then tells him to tear down the altar of Baal. Gideon is afraid to go during the day, so he goes at night. Then he questions again whether God will deliver Israel. This time he puts a lamb's fleece on the ground. If God will deliver Israel, then the lamb's fleece will be wet in the morning and the ground around it will be dry. The next morning it is so. That ought to satisfy him, right? Wrong! Wanting to be sure, and hoping that God won't get too mad, Gideon asks Him to do it again, but this time with the opposite results (i.e., the fleece dry and the ground wet). Not exactly the stuff heroes are made of. But God answers Gideon's request and then He reduces Gideon's army down to 300 men!

The whole point of the passage is that God, not a human person, is the deliverer. God chose a man desperately seeking assurance and reduced an army down to nothing so that the victory would clearly be His. The fleece wasn't a means of demonstrating faith; it was just the opposite. And it certainly wasn't used to determine God's will. God had already told Gideon what to do. Gideon was questioning the integrity of God, just as we do if we ask for a fleece when God has already shown us His will. "An evil and adulterous generation craves for a sign" (Matthew 12:39). As God's people, let's seek the face of God.

Your Position in Christ

Submit therefore to God. Resist the devil and he will flee from you.
JAMES 4:7

Daisy was a person who was caught in spiritual conflicts and suffered from demonic influences. She was a Christian and a university graduate, but she had severe mental and emotional problems which developed after her father divorced her mother. Within a period of five years Daisy had been institutionalized three times as a paranoid schizophrenic. After about three weeks of counseling with me, Daisy finally found the nerve to bring up the nighttime visitation of snakes.

"What about the snakes?" I asked.

"They crawl on me at night when I'm in bed," she confessed.

"What do you do when the snakes come?"

"I run in to my mother. But they always come back when I'm alone."

"Why don't you try something different," I continued. "When you're in bed and the snakes come, say out loud, 'In the name of Christ I command you to leave me.'"

"I couldn't do that," Daisy protested. "I'm not mature enough or strong enough."

"It's not a matter of your maturity; it's a matter of your position in Christ. You have as much right to resist Satan as I do."

Daisy squirmed at the prospect. "Well, I guess I could do that," Daisy sighed, sounding like she had just agreed to take castor oil.

The next week when Daisy walked in she said, "The snakes are gone!" If her problem had been strictly a neurological or chemical imbalance, taking authority over the snakes in Jesus' name wouldn't have worked. But in Daisy's case, the problem was spiritual.

James wrote: "Resist the devil and he will flee from you" (James 4:7). But if you don't resist him, he doesn't have to go. Or if you just pull the covers over your head in fear and say, "O God, do something about these demonic influences," the evil spirits don't have to leave. Resisting the devil is your responsibility based on the authority you possess in Christ.

We Have Been Saved

Christ, having appeared once to bear the sins of many,
will appear a second time, not to deal with sin but to
save those who are eagerly waiting for him.
HEBREWS 9:28 ESV

The word *salvation* in Scripture occurs in the past, present, and future tenses. Born-again believers have been saved, are being saved, and someday will be fully saved. "By grace you *have been saved* through faith" (Ephesians 2:8 ESV; see also 2 Timothy 1:8-9 and Titus 3:4-5). "Examine yourselves, to see whether you are in the faith. Test yourselves. Or do you not realize this about yourselves, that Jesus Christ is in you?—unless indeed you fail to meet the test!" (2 Corinthians 13:5 ESV). "This is the testimony, that God gave us eternal life, and this life is in his Son. Whoever has the Son has life; whoever does not have the Son of God does not have life. I write these things to you who believe in the name of the Son of God, that you may know that you have eternal life" (1 John 5:11-13 ESV).

"In him you also, when you heard the word of truth, the gospel of your salvation, and believed in him, were sealed with the promised Holy Spirit [past], who is the guarantee of our inheritance until we acquire possession of it [future]" (Ephesians 1:13-14 ESV). There can be no surer guarantee of the consummation of our salvation than the presence of God in our lives.

We have not yet experienced the totality of our salvation, and we won't until we are fully in the presence of God. On our way to heaven, we will face many obstacles that will challenge our faith. "Therefore, my beloved, as you have always obeyed, so now, not only as in my presence but much more in my absence, work out your own salvation with fear and trembling, for it is God who works in you, both to will and to work for his good pleasure" (Philippians 2:12-13 ESV).

We do not work for our salvation; we work out what God has born in us. And, we have the Holy Spirit, who empowers and guides us to our final destination.

The Laws of God

Now you Pharisees clean the outside of the cup and of the platter;
but inside of you, you are full of robbery and wickedness.
Luke 11:39

The *Talmud*, a collection of ancient rabbinic writings, relates the story of Rabbi Akiba, who was imprisoned. Rabbi Joshua brought him some water, but the guard spilled half of the container. There was too little water to both wash and drink, and Rabbi Akiba faced the possibility of death for lack of water if he chose to use the water for ceremonial washing. He reasoned, "He who eats with unwashed hands perpetuates a crime that ought to be punished by death. Better for me to die of thirst than to transgress the traditions of my ancestors!"

Jesus responded harshly to such reasoning: "You blind guides, who strain out a gnat and swallow a camel!" (Matthew 23:24). The Lord cautions that the weightier matters of the law (such as justice and mercy) are overlooked when attention focuses on strict observances of religious practices. This leads to a corresponding negligence of the eternal laws of God. Jesus told people to pay more attention to cleansing their hearts and not be like their leaders who cleanse only their hands.

The laws of God are liberating and protective. They are restrictive only when they protect us from the evil one. The rules of any institution should ensure the freedom of each individual to reach his or her God-given potential. They should serve as a guide so we don't stray from our purpose, and they should protect us from those who abuse the system.

The principle that Jesus modeled could be stated as follows: If people are commanded to follow a traditional practice that makes life more difficult and no longer contributes to the purpose of the organization, then we must not participate as a matter of religious conscience. Jesus simply didn't observe such traditions, and He defended His disciples for not observing them as well.

Don't You Know?

What shall we say then? Are we to continue in sin that grace may
abound? By no means! How can we who died to sin still live in it?
ROMANS 6:1-2 ESV

Wouldn't it make the pardoning of our sins even more magnani-
mous if we continued in our sinful ways? This is an absurd question that obscures the whole gospel. With the pardoning comes new life
that frees us from sin, not allowing us to continue in it. We were dead
in our trespasses and sin, but now we are alive and free in Christ.

Paul's argument in Romans 6:1-10 is based on what Christ has already
done for us—that which we could not do for ourselves. His victory over
sin and death is our victory because we are united to Him. Paul said,
"Know this," not "Do this." Our role is to believe.

Nobody can consistently behave in a way that is inconsistent with
what they believe about themselves. So Paul asks, "Do you not know
that all of us who have been baptized into Christ Jesus were baptized
into his death?" (Romans 6:3 ESV) (and His burial and resurrection—
verses 4-5). When we act contrary to who we are, we should ask ourselves, *Come on, don't you know the truth that set you free? Don't you know*
that you have been united to Christ in His death, burial, and resurrection?
Don't you know that you have been joined to God and committed yourself
to follow Him? Don't you know these things? Don't you know who you are?

We should regularly ask ourselves such questions and then reply with
conviction, *Yes, I do know who I am—a new creation in Christ. And by*
the grace of God, I shall live accordingly.

The Definition of Discipleship

Encourage one another, and build up one
another, just as you also are doing.
1 Thessalonians 5:11

Jesus' primary call to His disciples is seen in His words "Come to Me" (Matthew 11:28) and "Follow Me" (Matthew 4:19). Mark records: "He appointed twelve, that they might be with Him, and that He might send them out to preach, and to have authority to cast out the demons" (Mark 3:14-15). Notice that Jesus' relationship with His disciples preceded His assignment to them. Discipleship is the intensely personal activity of two or more persons helping each other experience a growing relationship with God. Discipleship is being before doing, maturity before ministry, character before career.

Every Christian, including you, is both a disciple and a discipler in the context of their Christian relationships. You have the awesome privilege and responsibility both to be a teacher and a learner of what it means to be in Christ, walk in the Spirit, and live by faith. You may have a role in your family, church, or Christian community which gives you specific responsibility for discipling others, such as husband/father, pastor, Sunday school teacher, discipleship group leader, etc. But even as an appointed discipler you are never not a disciple who is learning and growing in Christ through your relationships. Conversely, you may not have an "official" responsibility to disciple anyone, but you are never not a discipler. You have the opportunity to help your children, your friends, and other believers grow in Christ through your caring and committed relationship with them.

Similarly, every Christian is both a counselor and counselee in the context of their Christian relationships. A good counselor should be a good discipler, and a good discipler should be a good counselor. Biblically, they are the same role. Your level of maturity may dictate that you do a lot of Christian counseling. But there will still be times when you need to seek or receive the counsel of other Christians. There will never be a day when we don't need each other.

Salvation Is Regeneration

He has granted to us His precious and magnificent promises, in order
that by them you might become partakers of the divine nature.
2 PETER 1:4

What does the Bible specifically say about our nature? The Greek word for *nature* is used in this way only twice in the New Testament. Ephesians 2:1-3 describes the nature we all shared before we came to Christ: "And you were dead in your trespasses and sins...and were by nature children of wrath." What was your basic nature before you were born again spiritually? You and every other Christian "were by nature children of wrath," dead in sin, subject to Satan's power, living completely to fulfill sinful lusts and desires. This is the condition of every unbeliever today.

The second occurrence of the word is in 2 Peter 1:4, describing our nature after we came to Christ: "He has granted to us His precious and magnificent promises, in order that by them you might become partakers of the divine nature."

When you came into spiritual union with God through your new birth, you didn't *add* a new, divine nature to your old, sinful nature. You *exchanged* natures. Salvation isn't just a matter of God forgiving your sins and issuing you a pass to heaven when you die. Salvation is regeneration. God changed you from darkness to light, from sinner to saint. There is a newness about you that wasn't there before. If God hadn't changed your identity at salvation, you would be stuck with your old identity until you died. How could you expect to grow to maturity if you didn't start as a transformed child of God? Becoming a partaker of God's nature is fundamental to a Christian's identity and maturity.

We are no longer in Adam, we are in Christ. We can still choose to walk according to the flesh, but why should we want to? "You are not in the flesh but in the Spirit, if indeed the Spirit of God dwells in you. But if anyone does not have the Spirit of Christ, he does not belong to Him" (Romans 8:9).

The Power of His Presence

My presence will go with you, and I will give you rest.
EXODUS 33:14 ESV

God saddled Moses with the responsibility of leading His people to the Promised Land. Feeling overwhelmed by the responsibility, Moses asked God the two most important questions any spiritual leader can ask: *Who is going with me?* and *Will you please show me your ways "that I may know you in order to find favor in your sight?"* (Exodus 33:12-13 ESV). God's work done in God's way will never lack God's support. Trying to serve God in our own strength and resources will lead to burnout.

Wandering around in the wilderness for 40 years with no bathroom facilities is not anybody's idea of rest, and yet God did give Moses rest. The only way you can ascertain whether an event was restful is by how you feel when it's over. "Moses was 120 years old when he died. His eye was undimmed, and his vigor was unabated" (Deuteronomy 34:7 ESV). "There remains a Sabbath rest for the people of God, for whoever has entered God's rest has also rested from his works as God did from his" (Hebrews 4:9-10 ESV). The Sabbath rest is living by faith in the power of His presence. God has a way of bringing us to the end of our resources, and out of our brokenness we discover His. "Not by might, nor by power, but by my Spirit, says the LORD of hosts" (Zechariah 4:6 ESV).

Jesus' invitation to us is, "Come to me, all who labor and are heavy laden, and I will give you rest. Take my yoke upon you, and learn from me, for I am gentle and lowly of heart, and you will find rest for your souls. For my yoke is easy, and my burden is light" (Matthew 11:28-30 ESV).

An Entirely New Self

You were formerly darkness, but now you are light
in the Lord; walk as children of light.
EPHESIANS 5:8

Ephesians 5:8 describes the essential change of nature which occurs at salvation. It doesn't say you were *in* darkness; it says you *were* darkness. Darkness was your nature, your very essence, as an unbeliever. Nor does it say you are now in the light; it says you *are* light. God changed your basic nature from darkness to light. The issue in this passage is not improving your nature. Your new nature is already determined. The issue is learning to walk in harmony with your new nature.

Why do you need the nature of Christ within you? So you can *be* like Christ, not just *act* like Him. God has not given us the power to imitate Him. He has made us partakers of His nature so that we can actually *be* like Him. You don't become a Christian by acting like one. We are not on a performance basis with God. He doesn't say, "Here are My standards, now you measure up." He knows you can't solve the problem of an old sinful self by simply improving your behavior. He must change your nature, give you an entirely new self—the life of Christ in you—which is the grace you need to measure up to His standards.

That was the point of His message in the Sermon on the Mount: "Unless your righteousness surpasses that of the scribes and Pharisees, you shall not enter the kingdom of heaven" (Matthew 5:20). The scribes and Pharisees were the religious perfectionists of their day. They had external behavior down to a science, but their hearts were like the insides of a tomb: reeking of death. Jesus is only interested in creating new persons from the inside out by infusing in them a brand-new nature and creating in them a new self. Only after He changes your identity and makes you a partaker of His nature will you be able to change your behavior.

Single Vision

The eye is the lamp of the body. So, if your eye is healthy, your whole body will be full of light, but if your eye is bad, your whole body will be full of darkness. If then the light in you is darkness, how great is the darkness!
MATTHEW 6:22-23 ESV

Ancient tradition viewed the eyes as the windows through which light entered the body. If the eyes were in good condition, the whole body received the benefits that light bestows. But if there was something wrong with the eyes, the whole body was plunged into the darkness, which breeds disease.

A subtle nuance in this passage is pregnant with meaning. The "clear eye" is the one with a single vision, which Jesus clarifies in the next verse: "No one can serve two masters, for either he will hate the one and love the other, or he will be devoted to the one and despise the other. You cannot serve God and money" (Matthew 6:24 ESV). There will be no peace serving two masters. "For the love of money [not money itself] is a root of all kinds of evils. It is through this craving that some have wandered away from the faith and pierced themselves with many pangs" (1 Timothy 6:10 ESV).

Jesus calls us to serve God alone. When we have this single vision, the result is this: "You are the light of the world...Nor do people light a lamp and put it under a basket, but on a stand, and it gives light to all in the house. In the same way, let your light shine before others, so that they may see your good works and give glory to your Father who is in heaven" (Matthew 5:14-16 ESV).

We choose which master we will serve—God or the riches of this world. Whichever master we choose, by that master we shall be controlled.

Overpowering the Captors

How can anyone enter the strong man's house and carry
off his property, unless he first binds the strong man?
MATTHEW 12:29

A prime target for our authoritative prayer is the "strong man" mentioned in Matthew 12:29. Jesus was saying that you cannot rescue people from the bonds of spiritual blindness or demonic influence unless you first overpower their captors. Satan's power is already broken, but he will not let go of anything he thinks he can keep until we exercise the authority delegated to us by the Lord Jesus Christ.

When we pray we are not trying to persuade God to join us in *our* service for Him; prayer is the activity of joining God in His ministry. By faith we lay hold of the property in Satan's clutches which rightfully belongs to God, and we hold on until Satan turns loose. He will hold on to these people until we demand their release on the basis of our authority in Christ. Once Satan is bound through prayer, he must let go.

Understanding the spiritual nature of our world should have a profound effect on our evangelistic strategy. All too often we proclaim the virtues of Christianity to unbelievers like someone standing outside a prison compound proclaiming to the inmates the virtues of the outside world. But unless someone overpowers the prison guards and opens the gates, how can the prisoners experience the freedom we're telling them about? We must learn to bind the strong man before we will be able to rescue his prisoners.

Your Journey Toward Christ

The thief comes only to steal, and kill, and destroy.

JOHN 10:10

How do evil spirits interfere with our lives? Here is a simple illustration. Imagine that you are standing at one end of a long, narrow street lined on both sides with two-story row houses. At the other end of the street stands Jesus, and your Christian life is the process of walking down that long street of maturity toward Him. There is absolutely nothing in the street which can keep you from reaching Jesus. So, when you receive Christ, you fix your eyes on Him and start walking.

But since this world is still under the dominion of Satan, the row houses on either side of you are inhabited by beings who are committed to keeping you from reaching your goal. They have no power or authority to block your path or even slow your step, so they hang out of the windows and call to you, hoping to turn your attention away from your goal and disrupt your progress by tempting you, accusing you, and deceiving you.

What is the enemy's goal in having his demons jeer you, taunt you, lure you, and question you from the windows and doorways along your path? He wants you to slow down, stop, sit down, and if possible, give up your journey toward Christ. He wants to influence you to doubt your ability to believe and serve God. Remember: He has absolutely no power or authority to keep you from steadily progressing in your walk toward Christ. And he can never again own you, because you have been redeemed by Jesus Christ and you are forever in Him (1 Peter 1:18-19). But if he can get you to listen to the thoughts he plants in your mind, he can influence you. And if you allow him to influence you long enough through temptation, accusation, and deception, he can control you.

If I could influence you to believe a lie, could I control your life? Yes. Let's fix our eyes on Jesus, "the author and perfecter of faith" (Hebrews 12:2) and take "every thought captive to the obedience of Christ" (2 Corinthians 10:5).

The Last Adam

The first man Adam became a living being; the last Adam became a life-giving spirit.
1 CORINTHIANS 15:45 ESV

The first Adam was born both physically and spiritually alive, but he died spiritually when he sinned. The last Adam, Jesus, was also born physically and spiritually alive, but unlike the first Adam, Jesus never sinned, even though He was tempted in every way (Hebrews 4:15). God promised that redemption would come through the seed of a woman (Genesis 3:15; 17:19; Galatians 3:16). "Therefore the Lord himself will give you a sign. Behold, the virgin shall conceive and bear a son, and shall call his name Immanuel" (Isaiah 7:14 ESV).

For us to become a worm to save worms doesn't remotely compare to Jesus, "who emptied himself, by taking the form [*morphe*] of a servant, being born in the likeness of men" (Philippians 2:7 ESV). *Morphe* stresses the inner essence or reality of that with which it is associated. Though Jesus "was in the form [*morphe*] of God, [He] did not count equality with God a thing to be grasped" (verse 6 ESV). Jesus didn't strive to be God because He was and is God. He was in essence both man and God. Jesus was one person with two natures. Our Kinsman Redeemer was fully God while also fully human.

Scripture makes the doctrine of the Incarnation a test of orthodoxy. "By this you know the Spirit of God: every spirit that confesses that Jesus Christ has come in the flesh is from God, and every spirit that does not confess Jesus is not from God. This is the spirit of the antichrist, which you heard was coming and now is in the world already" (1 John 4:2-3 ESV). Satan knows who Jesus is and "has blinded the minds of the unbelievers, to keep them from seeing the light of the gospel of the glory of Christ, who is the image of God" (2 Corinthians 4:4 ESV).

Without the love of God, we would have never known the truth. Without the truth, we would never have known the love of God.

The Accuser of the Brethren

*The accuser of our brethren...who accuses them
before our God day and night.*

REVELATION 12:10

Next to temptation, perhaps the most frequent and insistent attack from Satan to which we are vulnerable is accusation. By faith we have entered into an eternal relationship with the Lord Jesus Christ. As a result, we are dead to sin and alive to God, and we now sit with Christ in the heavenlies. In Christ we are important, we are qualified, we are justified. Satan can do absolutely nothing to alter our position in Christ and our worth to God. But he can render us virtually inoperative if he can deceive us into listening to and believing his insidious lies accusing us of being of little value to God or other people.

Satan often uses temptation and accusation as a brutal one-two punch. He comes along and says, "Why don't you try it? Everybody does it. Besides, you can get away with it. Who's going to know?" Then as soon as we fall for his tempting line, he changes his tune to accusation: "What kind of a Christian are you to do such a thing? You're a pitiful excuse for a child of God. You'll never get away with it. You might as well give up because God has already given up on you."

We have all heard Satan's lying, hateful voice in our hearts and consciences. He never seems to let up on us. Many Christians are perpetually discouraged and defeated because they believe his persistent lies about them. And those who give in to his accusations end up being robbed of the freedom that God intends His people to enjoy.

The good news is we don't have to listen to Satan and live in despair and defeat. Satan is not your judge; he is merely your *accuser*. When Satan's accusations of unworthiness attack you, don't give heed. Instead respond, "I have put my trust in Christ, and I am a child of God in Him. I have been rescued by God from the fire of judgment, and He has declared me righteous. Satan cannot determine a verdict or pronounce a sentence. All he can do is accuse me—and I don't buy it."

A Struggling Saint

I am not practicing what I would like to do,
but I am doing the very thing I hate.

ROMANS 7:15

Perhaps the most vivid description of the contest with sin which goes on in the life of the believer is found in Romans 7:15-25. In verses 15 and 16, Paul describes the problem: "For that which I am doing, I do not understand; for I am not practicing what I would like to do, but I am doing the very thing I hate. But if I do the very thing I do not wish to do, I agree with the Law, confessing that it is good."

Notice that there is only one player in these two verses—the "I," mentioned nine times. Notice also that this person has a good heart; he agrees with the law of God. But this good-hearted Christian has a behavior problem. He knows what he should be doing but, for some reason, he can't do it. He agrees with God but ends up doing the very things he hates.

Verses 17-21 uncover the reason for this behavior problem: "So now, no longer am I the one doing it, but sin which indwells me…If I am doing the very thing I do not wish, I am no longer the one doing it, but sin which dwells in me." How many players are involved now? Two: sin and me. But sin is clearly not me; it's only dwelling in me. Sin is preventing me from doing what I want to do.

Do these verses say that I am no good, that I am evil, or that I am sin? Absolutely not. They say that I have something dwelling in me which is no good, evil, and sinful, but it's not me. If I have a sliver in my finger, I could say that I have something in me which is no good. But it's not me who's no good. I'm not the sliver. The sliver which is stuck in my finger is no good. I am not sin and I am not a sinner. I am a saint struggling with sin which causes me to do what I don't want to do.

Romans 6:12 informs us that it is our responsibility not to allow sin to reign in our lives. Sin will reign if we use our bodies as instruments of unrighteousness (Romans 6:13). We must renounce every such use and submit our bodies to God as instruments of righteousness.

Mature Thinking

Brothers, do not be children in your thinking.
Be infants in evil, but in your thinking be mature.
1 CORINTHIANS 14:20 ESV

On Monday, a longtime employee finds a note from his boss on his desk asking him to come to his office on Friday at 10:00 a.m. The company has been downsizing, so he can't help but wonder why he's being summoned. At first he thinks he's going to be laid off after years of faithful service, and he becomes angry. Anger is about control or the absence of it. Then he thinks, *Maybe I'm not. But then again, maybe I am—or not!* Now he's anxious, because "he is a double-minded man, unstable in all his ways" (James 1:8 ESV). *Anxiety* (*merimna* in the Greek) is a combination of *merizo* ("divide") and *nous* ("mind"). People are anxious because they don't know what's going to happen next. By Thursday the employee has convinced himself that he's going to be laid off, and he wonders how he can start over again at his age.

Now he's depressed, feeling hopeless and helpless. Counselors have observed that depressed people have a negative view of themselves, their present circumstances, and the future. Friday comes, and he's an emotional wreck when he walks into the boss's office. "Congratulations," his boss says. "We've made you vice-president." Now how does he feel?

The anger, anxiety, and depression were all a product of his thoughts. If what we believe doesn't conform to truth, then what we feel doesn't conform to reality. People are doing what they are doing and feeling what they are feeling because of what they have chosen to think and believe. Therefore, we should be mature in what we think and certain of what we believe.

Be God-Centered

Jesus called the twelve together, and gave them power and authority
over all the demons, and to heal diseases. And He sent them out
to proclaim the kingdom of God, and to perform healing.

LUKE 9:1-2

Notice how Jesus equipped His disciples for ministry. He knew that when they began preaching the kingdom of God and healing the sick, demonic powers would bring opposition. So He specifically gave them power and authority over demons.

Later, Jesus sent out 70 of His followers on a similar mission, and they "returned with joy, saying, 'Lord, even the demons are subject to us in Your name'" (Luke 10:17). These missionaries were spiritually in tune enough to know that demons existed and that they were a force to be reckoned with in their ministry. Jesus' followers had been eyewitnesses as the evil spirits opposed the Master, and they probably anticipated the same treatment. Perhaps they even started out on their mission with pangs of fear and doubt about encountering demonic resistance. But they came back astonished at the victory they experienced over evil spirits.

But Jesus quickly brought the issue of spiritual conflicts into perspective: "Do not rejoice in this, that the spirits are subject to you, but rejoice that your names are recorded in heaven" (Luke 10:20). Jesus sent out the 70 to preach the gospel and to heal, but all they could talk about when they came back was how they sent the demons running. The nature of Jesus' response was: "Don't be demon-centered. Be kingdom-centered, be ministry-centered, be God-centered."

That's a good warning. As you learn to exercise authority over the kingdom of darkness in your life and in the lives of others, you may be tempted to see yourself as some kind of spiritual freedom fighter, looking for demons behind every door. But it's truth which sets you free, not the knowledge of error. You are not called to dispel the darkness; you are called to turn on the light. You would have no authority at all if it weren't for your identity as a child of God and your position in Christ.

Free to Live

If you are led by the Spirit, you are not under the Law.
GALATIANS 5:18

Paul said that walking according to the Spirit is not license: an excessive or undisciplined freedom constituting an abuse of privilege. As a Christian you may see the phrase "You are not under the Law" in Galatians 5:18 and exclaim, "Wow, I'm free! Walking in the Spirit means I can do anything I want!" Not at all. In the previous verse Paul wrote, "You may not do the things that you please." Being led by the Spirit doesn't mean you are free to do anything you want to do. It means you are finally free to live a responsible, moral life—something you were incapable of doing when you were the prisoner of your flesh.

Once I was invited to speak to a religion class at a Catholic high school on the topic of Protestant Christianity. At the end of my talk, an athletic-looking, streetwise student raised his hand and asked, "Do you have a lot of don'ts in your church?"

Sensing that he had a deeper motive, I answered, "What you really want to ask me is if we have any freedom, right?" He nodded.

"Sure, I'm free to do whatever I want to do," I answered. "I'm free to rob a bank. But I'm mature enough to realize that I would be in bondage to that act for the rest of my life. I'd have to cover up my crime, go into hiding, or eventually pay for what I did. I'm also free to tell a lie. But if I do, I have to keep telling it, and I have to remember who I told it to and how I told it or I will get caught. I'm free to do drugs, abuse alcohol, and live a sexually immoral lifestyle. All of those 'freedoms' lead to bondage. I'm free to make those choices, but considering the consequences, would I really be free?"

What appears to be freedom to some people isn't really freedom, but a return to bondage (Galatians 5:1). God's laws, from which we seek to be free, are not restrictive, but protective. Your real freedom is your ability to choose to live responsibly within the context of the protective guidelines God has established for our lives.

Freed from Legalism

God...made us adequate as servants of a new covenant, not of the letter, but of the Spirit; for the letter kills, but the Spirit gives life.
2 CORINTHIANS 3:5-6

Walking by the Spirit is not legalism, the opposite extreme from license. Paul said: "If you are led by the Spirit, you are not under the Law" (Galatians 5:18). Stringently striving to obey Christian rules and regulations doesn't enable the Spirit-filled walk; it often kills it (2 Corinthians 3:6). We're told in Galatians 3:13 that the law is really a curse, and in Galatians 3:21 that it is impotent, powerless to give life.

Laying down the law—telling someone that it is wrong to do this or that—does not give them the power to stop doing it. Christians have been notorious at trying to legislate spirituality with don'ts: Christians don't drink, don't smoke, don't dance, don't attend movies, don't play cards, don't wear makeup, etc. But legalism can't curb immorality. In fact, laying down the law merely serves to heighten the temptation. Paul said that the law actually stimulates the desire to do what it forbids (Romans 7:5)! When you tell your child not to cross a certain line, where does he immediately want to go? Forbidden fruit often seems to be the most desirable.

Neither will a Spirit-filled heart be produced by demanding that someone conform to a religious code of behavior. We often equate Christian disciplines such as Bible study, prayer, regular church attendance, and witnessing with spiritual maturity. All these activities are good and helpful for spiritual growth. But merely performing these admirable Christian exercises does not guarantee a Spirit-filled walk.

Does this mean that establishing rules is wrong? Of course not. God's law is a necessary protective moral standard and guideline. But the means by which we live a life of freedom is not the law but grace. Within the confines of God's law we are free to nurture a spirit-to-Spirit relationship with God, which is the essence of walking in the Spirit.

Free to Choose

The Lord is the Spirit; and where the Spirit of the Lord is, there is liberty.

2 CORINTHIANS 3:17

The Spirit-filled walk is neither characterized by license nor legalism, but liberty. Paul stated that we are "servants of a new covenant, not of the letter, but of the Spirit; for the letter kills, but the Spirit gives life...Now the Lord is the Spirit; and where the Spirit of the Lord is, there is liberty" (2 Corinthians 3:6, 17).

I believe that our freedom in Christ is one of the most precious commodities we have received from our spiritual union with God. Because the Spirit of the Lord is in you, you are free to choose to live a responsible and moral life. You are no longer compelled to walk according to the flesh as you were before conversion. And now you are not even compelled to walk according to the Spirit. You are free to choose to walk according to the Spirit or to walk according to the flesh.

Walking according to the Spirit implies two things. First, it's not passive. We're talking about *walking* in the Spirit, not *sitting* in the Spirit. One of the most dangerous and harmful detriments to your spiritual growth is passivity—putting your mind in neutral and coasting. The Christian classic *War on the Saints,* by Jessie Penn-Lewis, was written to combat such passive thinking. Sitting back and waiting for God to do everything is not God's way to spiritual maturity.

Second, we're talking about *walking* in the Spirit, not *running* in the Spirit. The Spirit-filled life is not achieved through endless, exhausting activity. We mistakenly think that the harder we work for God, the more spiritual we will become. That's a subtle lie from the enemy. Satan knows that he may not be able to stop you from serving God by making you immoral, but he can probably impede your service by simply making you busy. Our service for God can become the greatest detriment of our devotion to God.

Forgiving Others

*Let all bitterness and wrath and anger and clamor and slander be
put away from you, along with all malice. Be kind to one another,
tenderhearted, forgiving one another, as God in Christ forgave you.*

EPHESIANS 4:31-32 ESV

Christ forgave us by taking the consequences for our sins on Himself. When we forgive another person, we're agreeing to live with
the consequences of that person's sin. *But that's not fair!* Of course it's
not, but you will have to live with them anyway. Everyone is living
with the consequences of somebody else's sin. The whole world is living with the consequences of Adam's sin. The only real choice is to
do that in the bondage of bitterness or in the freedom of forgiveness.
There has been enough pain; choose forgiveness. It's the most Christlike thing we can do.

To forgive another is to set a captive free and to realize that you were
the captive. What is to be gained is freedom from your past. *But where
is the justice?* Justice is the cross. Jesus died for your sins and everyone
else's. *I'll wait until I heal first; then maybe I'll forgive.* That will never
happen, because you forgive so you will heal. Jesus came to set captives
free and to heal the brokenhearted. In this world you will not have perfect justice, but God will make it right in the end. To err is human, but
to forgive is divine.

We don't forgive others for their sake; we do it for the sake of our own
freedom and our relationship with our heavenly Father. It's primarily an
issue between ourselves and God, and we can forgive anytime, like right
now. To forgive from the heart, we have to let God into our emotional
core. Ask Him to reveal whom you need to forgive. As names come to
mind, say, *Lord, I forgive* [name] *for* [specifically mention every hurtful
thing that comes to mind and how it made you feel, such as worthless,
rejected, unloved, dirty, embarrassed].

Seeking Forgiveness

If you are offering your gift at the altar and there remember that your brother has something against you, leave your gift there before the altar and go. First be reconciled to your brother, and then come and offer your gift.

MATTHEW 5:23-24 ESV

If someone has hurt you, don't go to them; go to God. You can't go to those who have died but you still need to forgive, and it's inadvisable to go to those who have abused you. It could lead to further abuse. However, if you have offended someone else, don't continue religious observances in hypocrisy when God has brought that person to your mind. Go to that person and seek their forgiveness, hoping for reconciliation, and pay for damages if called for.

Don't document it for legal reasons or send a letter or email unless that is the only way to communicate. Go in person and say, "Would you forgive me for [specifically say what you did without explanation or rationalization]." It's manipulative to do that hoping they will own up to the sins they have committed. Whether they forgive you or not is their choice. If they choose not to forgive you, you aren't obligated to do anything more—unless you need to pay for the damage that was done. Then go to church with a clear conscience. Paul said, "I always take pains to have a clear conscience toward both God and man" (Acts 24:16 ESV).

Hear His Voice

He is our God, and we are the people of his pasture, and the sheep of
his hand. Today, if you hear his voice, do not harden your hearts.

PSALM 95:7-8 ESV

Often, quiet times with God aren't quiet. Our thoughts are distracted and even riddled with temptations directed at our vulnerabilities. We're hearing from everybody but God—or at least it seems that way. Maybe God is allowing that to get our attention, but in reality we are hearing from Him.

If you have a rebellious child who is always asking for one thing or another, what's on your mind, Mom or Dad? What would you like to talk to your child about? If any unresolved issues are between you and your heavenly Father, be assured that is what will be on your mind during quiet times. That is why the psalmist said, "Do not harden your hearts."

Nothing is more important than our relationship with God. He wants to remove the barriers that are keeping us from having an intimate relationship with Him. A good way to assess the intimacy of our relationship with God is to get totally alone and see how well we tolerate solitude. God declares through the psalmist, "Be still, and know that I am God" (Psalm 46:10 ESV). Can we sit peacefully in His presence with a quiet mind and not feel obligated to say or do something?

Rather than see an unresolved issue as a distraction, make it the subject of your prayer, which should lead to confession, repentance, and a new direction for life. Don't be deceived and think, *I can't talk to God about that.* He already knows about it, so why not be honest with Him? It just may set you free and give you peace.

In Christ

Truly, truly, I say to you, unless one is born again,
he cannot see the kingdom of God.
JOHN 3:3

Being in Christ, and all that it means to Christian maturity and freedom, is the overwhelming theme of the New Testament. For example, in the six chapters of the book of Ephesians alone there are 40 references to being in Christ and having Christ in you. For every reference to Christ being in you there are ten to you being in Christ. Being in Christ is the most critical element of our identity.

But we weren't born in Christ. We were born in sin, thanks to the first Adam. What is God's plan for transforming us from being in Adam to being in Christ? We must be born again (John 3:3). Physical birth only gains us physical life. Spiritual life, the eternal life Christ promises to those who come to Him, is only gained through spiritual birth (John 3:36).

What does it mean to be spiritually alive in Christ? The moment you were born again your soul came into union with God in the same way Adam was in union with God before the Fall. Your spiritual union with God is complete and eternal because it is provided by Christ, the last Adam. As long as Christ remains alive spiritually, you will remain alive spiritually—and that's for eternity.

Contrary to what many Christians believe, eternal life is not something you get when you die. You are spiritually alive in Christ right now. That's how you got to be in union with God, by being born again spiritually. You'll never be more spiritually alive than you are right now. The only thing that will change when you die physically is that you will exchange your old earthbound body for a new one. But your spiritual life in Christ, which began when you personally trusted Him, will merely continue on.

Eternal life is something you possess right now because you're in Christ. Believe it. Rejoice in it.

Conforming to the Image of God
For this is the will of God, your sanctification.

1 THESSALONIANS 4:3

In a personal sense, God's will for our lives is that we conform to the image of God, something the apostle Paul makes clear in 1 Thessalonians 4:3: "For this is the will of God, your sanctification." In his letter to Roman Christians, Paul writes, "For whom He foreknew, He also predestined to become conformed to the image of His Son" (Romans 8:29) and adds in 1 Timothy 1:5, "The goal of our instruction is love from a pure heart and a good conscience and a sincere faith." God's will for our lives is to become the person God intended us to be.

There is no instruction in the Bible concerning career choice, where we live, or who we should marry. However, God does provide guidance for those who are living out His will. There is an abundance of instruction on how we're to relate to our employer and behave on the job we already have (Colossians 3:22-25). And there is much about how to relate with one another (Colossians 3:10-14) and live with our families (Colossians 3:18-21).

The Bible overwhelmingly instructs that to do God's will means living in harmony with God and others: "'You shall love the LORD your God with all your heart, and with all your soul, and with all your mind.' This is the great and foremost commandment. And a second is like it, 'You shall love your neighbor as yourself.' On these two commandments depend the whole Law and the Prophets" (Matthew 22:37-40).

The whole purpose of the Bible is to teach us how to have a relationship with God and live in harmony with one another. We do this by assuming our responsibilities for today and trusting God for tomorrow.

I'm not sure the Lord cares primarily whether you are a carpenter, teacher, or doctor. But He does care what kind of carpenter, teacher, or doctor you are. Determine to be the person He has called you to be and you will fulfill your purpose and calling.

Put Up This Sail!

*The wind blows where it wishes and you hear the sound
of it, but do not know where it comes from and where it
is going; so is everyone who is born of the Spirit.*

John 3:8

What does it take to be the selfless, loving Christian we desire to be? What is needed to move us beyond our inconsequential selfish, fleshly pursuits to deeds of loving service to God and others?

First, it requires a firm grasp on your identity in Christ. You can't love like Jesus loved until you accept the reality that, since you are in Christ, His divine nature is united with your spirit.

Second, you must believe that the old sin-trained flesh has been crucified with Christ (Galatians 2:20; 6:14) and walk in accordance with who you are: a child of God united with God's Spirit.

The fact that the Holy Spirit resides in us and that we can live according to His leading is an awesome but elusive concept to many. The problem is not new. Nicodemus was a learned man, but he couldn't comprehend life in the Spirit. So Jesus told him, "The wind blows where it wishes and you hear the sound of it, but do not know where it comes from and where it is going; so is everyone who is born of the Spirit" (John 3:8). Trying to reduce life in the Spirit to a formula is like trying to capture the wind.

Someone reflecting on the mysteries of walking by the Spirit said, "I think we need to pull in the oars and put up the sail!" I like that. When we walk by the Spirit, we stop striving. We are no longer driven; we are led. "For all who are being led by the Spirit of God, these are sons of God" (Romans 8:14). When we come to the end of our resources, we discover His.

God's Feedback System

"For I know the plans that I have for you," declares the L<small>ORD</small>, *"plans for welfare and not for calamity to give you a future and a hope."*
J<small>EREMIAH</small> 29:11

I believe that God desires all His children to be successful, significant, fulfilled, satisfied, joyful, secure, and to live in peace. From birth you have been developing in your mind a means for experiencing these values and reaching other goals in life. Consciously or subconsciously you continue to formulate and adjust your plans for achieving these goals.

But sometimes your well-intended plans and noble-sounding goals are not completely in harmony with God's plans and goals for you. *How can I know if what I believe is right?* you may be wondering. *Must I wait until I am 45 years old or until I experience some kind of mid-life crisis to discover that what I believed was wrong?* I don't think so. I believe that God has designed us in such a way that we can know on a regular basis if our belief system is properly aligned with God's truth. God has established a feedback system which is designed to grab your attention so you can examine the validity of your goal.

That system is your emotions. When an experience or relationship leaves you feeling angry, anxious, or depressed, those emotional signposts are there to alert you that you may be cherishing a faulty goal which is based on a wrong belief. If our goals are blocked, we become angry. If our goals are uncertain, we feel anxious. If we perceive our goals as impossible, we become depressed because the heart of depression is hopelessness.

Can any God-given goal be blocked, uncertain, or impossible? Put another way, if God wants something done, can it be done? Of course! The question is, do we have a biblical understanding of success, significance, fulfillment, satisfaction, joy, security, and peace? When we see and pursue these values from God's perspective, we will reach our goals because they are God's goals for us.

Emotional Honesty

*Having put away falsehood, let each one of you speak the
truth with his neighbor, for we are members one of another.
Be angry and do not sin; do not let the sun go down on
your anger, and give no opportunity to the devil.*

EPHESIANS 4:25-27 ESV

Your emotions are to your soul what your physical feelings are to your body. Nobody in their right mind enjoys pain. But if you didn't feel pain, you would be in danger of serious injury and infection. And if you didn't feel anger, sorrow, joy, etc., your soul would be in trouble. Emotions are God's gauges to let you know what is going on inside. They are neither good nor bad; they're amoral, just part of your humanity. Just like you respond to the warnings of physical pain, so you need to learn to respond to your emotional signals.

Emotions can be thought of like an indicator light on the dash of a car. Covering up the irritating light with tape is suppression. Breaking the light with a hammer is indiscriminate expression. Looking under the hood is acknowledgment. Suppression is dishonest and unhealthful. We communicate verbally and nonverbally, and when they don't match, we believe the nonverbal.

It is a falsehood to say something incongruent with what we are actually feeling. The sin is not being angry; it's being dishonest about being angry but failing to "look under the hood." Being emotionally honest and speaking the truth in love makes for healthy relationships. Bottled up emotions are the basis for many psychosomatic illnesses. "When I kept silent [about my sin], my bones wasted away" (Psalm 32:3 ESV). Indiscriminate expression may be healthier for us, but potentially harmful to the other person. "Let every person be quick to hear, slow to speak, slow to anger; for the anger of man does not produce the righteousness of God" (James 1:19-20 ESV). Therefore, "confess [acknowledge/be honest about] your sins to one another and pray for one another, that you may be healed" (5:16 ESV).

A Heart for God

Hear, O Israel: The LORD our God, the LORD is one. You shall love the LORD your God with all your heart and with all your soul and with all your might. And these words I command you today shall be on your heart.

DEUTERONOMY 6:4-6 ESV

The above passage is referred to as the *Shema* (from the first word, *Hear*), which began Judaism's confession of faith. *Shema* meant to hear as though to obey. It was to be taught by the people to their children throughout the day. They were instructed to "bind them as a sign on your hand, and they shall be as frontlets between your eyes" (Deuteronomy 6:8 ESV). That probably referred to all that you think and do, but Orthodox Jews practiced this commandment by wearing phylacteries—small boxes containing scriptures worn on their heads and arms during prayer.

The heart is the center of self. Only in the heart do the mind, will, and emotions converge. Intellectual knowledge of a subject may not have any impact on our lives unless the truth enters our hearts. When it does, we are emotionally affected, and that drives the will. Thinking, feeling, and willing all come together here in holistic unity. In the Bible, to "know" something is to grasp it such that it affects the total personality. For instance, "Adam knew Eve his wife, and she conceived and bore Cain" (Genesis 4:1 ESV). The heart is the place where God addresses us and from which we respond with all our hearts.

To make worship a holistic expression of the heart, the early church adopted practices that included all the senses—such as liturgy that is sung, incense, candles, bells, and icons that tell a biblical story. Such practices are still carried on by the Orthodox Church around the world, making worship a meaningful experience.

No Longer Under Obligation

Our old self was crucified with Him, that our body of sin might
be done away with, that we should no longer be slaves to sin.

ROMANS 6:6

Why did the old self need to die? The old self was independent and disobedient to God, so it had to die in order that "our body of sin might be done away with, that we should no longer be slaves to sin" (Romans 6:6). Death is the ending of a relationship, but not of existence. Sin hasn't died; it is still strong and appealing. But when your old self died with Christ on the cross, your relationship with sin ended forever. You are no longer "in the flesh" but "in Christ" (Romans 8:9). Your old self (the sinner) and your old nature (characterized by the sin which was inevitable since you were separated from God) are gone forever because you are no longer separated from God.

Does this mean that you are now sinless? By no means. The death of your old self formally ended your relationship with sin, but it did not end sin's existence. Sin and Satan are still around, and they are strong and appealing. But by virtue of the crucifixion of the old self, sin's power over you is broken (Romans 6:7, 12, 14). You are no longer under any obligation to serve sin, to obey sin, or to respond to sin.

You commit sin when you willfully allow yourself to act independently of God as the old self did as a matter of course. When you function in this manner you are violating your new nature and your new identity. Such actions must be confessed and forsaken.

Even though the old self, which you were in Adam, is dead, you still have to contend with the flesh. The way you learned to live your life before Christ is still programmed into your mind. Knowing that your old self was crucified with Christ makes it possible for you to choose not to sin. You no longer have to walk after the flesh; you may now walk after the Spirit. You are free.

The Spirit's Conviction

I now rejoice, not that you were made sorrowful, but that
you were made sorrowful to the point of repentance; for you
were made sorrowful according to the will of God.

2 CORINTHIANS 7:9

I'm often asked, "How can I tell the difference between the devil's accusations and the Holy Spirit's conviction?" Every Christian is faced with the choice of walking by the Spirit or by the flesh on a daily basis. The moment you choose to walk according to the flesh, the Holy Spirit brings conviction because what you have just chosen to do is not compatible with who you really are. If you continue in the flesh, you will feel the sorrow of conviction.

"How do I know which kind of sorrow I'm experiencing?" you may ask. "The devil's accusation and the Spirit's conviction both make me feel sorrowful." Determine whether your feelings reflect thoughts of truth or error, and you will identify their source. Do you feel guilty, worthless, stupid, or inept? That's a sorrow provoked by accusation because those feelings don't reflect truth. Judicially, you are no longer guilty; you have been justified through your faith in Christ, and there is no condemnation for those who are in Christ. You are not worthless; Jesus gave His life for you. You are not stupid or inept; you can do all things through Christ. When you find lies lurking beneath your feelings of sorrow—especially if your feelings persistently drive you into the ground—you are being falsely accused. To disarm the sorrow of accusation you must submit yourself to God and resist the devil and his lies.

But if you are sorrowful because your behavior doesn't reflect your true identity in Christ, that's the sorrow according to the will of God which is designed to produce repentance. It's the Holy Spirit calling you to admit on the basis of 1 John 1:9, "Dear Lord, I was wrong." As soon as you confess and repent, God says, "I'm glad you shared that with Me. You're cleansed; now get on with life." And you walk away from that confrontation free. The sorrow is gone, and you have a positive new resolve to obey God in the area of your failure.

Accusation and Conviction

The sorrow that is according to the will of God produces a repentance without regret, leading to salvation; but the sorrow of the world produces death.

2 CORINTHIANS 7:10

A graphic example of the contrast between accusation and conviction is found in the lives of Judas Iscariot and Simon Peter. Somehow Judas allowed Satan to deceive him into betraying Jesus for 30 pieces of silver (Luke 22:3-5). When Judas realized what he had done, he was so remorseful that he hung himself. Was his suicide the result of Satan's accusation or of God's conviction? It had to be accusation because it drove Judas to kill himself. Accusation leads to death; conviction leads to repentance and life.

Peter also failed Jesus by denying Him. It apparently began with pride as the disciples argued over who was the greatest among them (Luke 22:24-30). Jesus told Peter, "Simon, Simon, behold, Satan has demanded permission to sift you like wheat" (verse 31). That's right—Jesus allowed Satan to put Peter through the mill because Peter had given the enemy a foothold through pride. But Jesus also looked at Peter and said, "I have prayed for you, that your faith may not fail; and you, when once you have turned again, strengthen your brothers" (verse 32).

Peter vowed to die with Jesus, but Jesus told him that he would deny Him three times (verses 33-34), which he did. The remorse Peter felt was every bit as painful as that which Judas experienced. But Peter's sorrow was from conviction which led to his eventual repentance and restoration to Christ (John 21:15-17). When your feelings of remorse drive you from God, you are being accused by Satan. Resist it. But when your sorrow draws you to confront Christ and confess your wrong, you are being convicted by the Spirit. Yield to it through repentance.

According to Revelation 12:10, Satan's continuing work is to accuse the brethren. But the good news is that Christ's continuing work is to intercede for us as He did for Peter (Hebrews 7:25). We have a persistent adversary, but we have an even more persistent, eternal advocate who defends us before the Father on the basis of our faith in Him (1 John 2:1).

What God Has Provided

If anyone thinks he is something when he is nothing, he deceives himself.
GALATIANS 6:3

Satan promotes his lies in the world by encouraging us to self-deception. We deceive ourselves when we think we are something we are not. The Scriptures instruct us not to think of ourselves more highly than we ought to think. "But I know who I am," you say. "I'm a child of God, I'm seated with Christ in the heavenlies, I can do all things through Him. That makes me pretty special." Yes, you are very special in the eyes of God. But you are what you are by the grace of God (1 Corinthians 15:10). The life you live, the talents you possess, and the gifts you have received are not personal accomplishments; they are expressions of God's grace. Never take credit for what God has provided; rather, take delight in accomplishing worthwhile deeds which glorify the Lord.

Furthermore, we deceive ourselves when we think we are wise in this age (1 Corinthians 3:18-19). It is the height of intellectual arrogance to assume wisdom without the revelation of God. "Professing to be wise, they became fools" (Romans 1:22). Sometimes we are tempted to think we can match wits and intellect with the god of this world. But we are no match for him. Whenever we think we can outsmart Satan on our own, we are prime candidates to be led astray by his craftiness.

However, Satan is no match for God. It is important for us not to lean on our own understanding, but to employ the mind of Christ and acknowledge Him in all our ways (Proverbs 3:5-6; 1 Corinthians 2:16). We overcome the lies of Satan by divine revelation, not human research or reasoning. Satan is not impressed with our intellect; he is defeated by God's omniscience.

Seated with Christ

*God…made us alive together with Christ (by grace you
have been saved), and raised us up with Him, and seated
us with Him in the heavenly places, in Christ Jesus.*

EPHESIANS 2:4-6

The New Testament clearly reveals that Christ's power and authority over Satan and his kingdom have been conferred to those of us
who are in Christ. In Ephesians 2:4-6 Paul explains that when Christ
was raised from the dead, those of us who have believed in Him were
also resurrected from our condition of spiritual death and made alive
"together with Christ." It's only logical that the head (Christ) and the
body (His church) should be raised together.

Furthermore, when God seated Christ at His right hand and conferred on Him all authority (Ephesians 1:20-21), He also seated us at His
right hand and conferred on us through Christ all authority because we
are "together with Christ." The moment you receive Christ, you take
possession of what God did for you 2,000 years ago. Your identity as
a child of God and your authority over spiritual powers are not things
you *are* receiving or *will* receive at some time in the future; you have
them right now. You are a spiritually-alive child of God *right now*. You
are seated in the heavenlies with Christ *right now*. You have power and
authority over the kingdom of darkness *right now*. We have the authority because of our position in Christ, and we have the power when we
are filled with the Holy Spirit.

Paul also related this life-changing truth in his letter to the Colossians: "In Him [Christ] you have been made complete, and He is the
head over all rule and authority" (Colossians 2:10). Notice again that
the action is past tense: We *have been* made complete. When? At the
death, resurrection, and ascension of Jesus Christ. And since Christ is
the God-appointed head over all rule and authority, and since we are
seated with Him in the heavenlies, we have the authority and power to
live responsible lives.

Lawlessness

Not everyone who says to me, "Lord, Lord," will enter the kingdom
of heaven, but the one who does the will of my Father who is in
heaven. On that day many will say to me, "Lord, Lord, did we not
prophesy in your name, and cast out demons in your name, and do
many mighty works in your name?" And then will I declare to them,
"I never knew you; depart from me, you workers of lawlessness."
MATTHEW 7:21-23 ESV

Prior to the above passage, Jesus said, "Beware of false prophets, who come to you in sheep's clothing but inwardly are ravenous wolves. You will recognize them by their fruits" (Matthew 7:15-16 ESV). Then He talks about some who appear to be bearing fruit, but says of them, "I never knew you."

False prophets are inspired by demons and speak falsely. They are puppets of Satan who oppose the will of God. "Such men are false apostles, deceitful workmen, disguising themselves as apostles of Christ. And no wonder, for even Satan disguises himself as an angel of light. So it is no surprise if his servants, also, disguise themselves as servants of righteousness. Their end will correspond to their deeds" (2 Corinthians 11:13-15 ESV).

Until the lawless nature of false prophets is exposed, we have to be spiritually discerning. True believers do the will of God and exhibit the fruit of righteousness, which the evil one will try to imitate but cannot duplicate.

Living Today

What sort of people ought you to be in holy conduct and godliness.

2 PETER 3:11

I believe in setting goals and making plans. But a biblical vision for the future and godly goals for ministry or work have no value if they don't provide direction for our steps today. Goals for tomorrow that don't prioritize present activities are nothing more than wishful thinking. We make plans for tomorrow in order to establish meaningful activities for today. We need to ask the Lord each day if we are still on target, and give Him the right to order midcourse changes in direction.

Some people don't like to set goals because they feel goals only set them up for failure. But a goal should never be a god. It should be a target, not a whip. Other people become obsessed with goals for tomorrow. Biblically, the will of God is almost entirely directed at living responsibly today. Legitimate goalsetting should support that.

Are you trying to tell us that we aren't to make any plans for the future or establish any goals for our ministry or work? No, I'm trying to say that the primary focus of God's will is that we seek to establish His kingdom by becoming the person He wants us to be *today*.

Most people want to know what God has in store for them tomorrow. That's why prophecy has always been a popular subject. Most prophecy teachers know that the critical issue concerning the Lord's second coming is, "What sort of people ought you to be in holy conduct and godliness" (2 Peter 3:11). Jesus said, "But seek first His kingdom and His righteousness; and all these things shall be added to you. Therefore do not be anxious for tomorrow" (Matthew 6:33-34). Biblical prophecy is given to us as a hope (the present assurance of some future good) so we will have the courage to live righteously and confidently today.

Feelings of Anger

*Let all bitterness and wrath and anger and clamor and
slander be put away from you, along with all malice.*

Ephesians 4:31

Feelings of anger should prompt us to reexamine what we believe and the mental goals we have formulated to accomplish those beliefs. My daughter Heidi helped me with this process one Sunday morning while I was trying to hustle my family out the door for church. I had been waiting in the car for several minutes before I stomped back into the house and shouted angrily, "We should have left for church 15 minutes ago!"

All was silent for a moment, then Heidi's soft voice floated around the corner from her bedroom: "What's the matter, Dad? Did somebody block your goal?" She was blocking my goal to get to church on time, but she wasn't blocking my goal to be the husband and father God wants me to be. The only one who can block that goal is me.

A wife and mother may say, "My goal in life is to have a loving, harmonious, happy family." Who can block that goal? Every person in her family can—not only *can*, they *will*! A homemaker clinging to the belief that her sense of worth is dependent on her family will crash and burn every time her husband or children fail to live up to her image of family harmony. She will probably be very angry, which could drive family members even farther away from her and each other. Her major goal in life should be to become the wife and mother God called her to be.

A pastor may say, "My goal in ministry is to reach this community for Christ." Good goal? It is a wonderful desire, but if his sense of worth is dependent on that desire being fulfilled, he will experience tremendous emotional turmoil. Every person in the community can block his goal. Pastors who continue to believe that their success is dependent on others will end up fighting with their boards, praying their opposition out of the church, or quitting.

Make it your goal to be what God has called you to be. No one can keep you from reaching that goal but you.

Dealing with Anxiety

*The peace of God, which surpasses all comprehension, shall
guard your hearts and your minds in Christ Jesus.*

PHILIPPIANS 4:7

Christians have frequently relied upon a sense of peace as evidence
of the Holy Spirit's leading. It is common to hear people say, "I
just don't have a peace about it." I think that is legitimate. I would be
concerned about the person who proceeds when his spirit is disturbed.
God doesn't lead through anxiety. We are to cast our anxiety upon Jesus,
because He cares for us (1 Peter 5:7).

Still, a lot of money is spent on the temporary "cure" of anxiety. People consume alcohol, take illegal drugs, turn to the refrigerator, have
sex, mindlessly repeat mantras, and escape to cabins, boats, and motor
homes—all to reduce their anxiety. One lady said, "Whenever I feel
anxious, I go on a shopping spree!" Prescription drugs are regularly dis-
pensed for the ails brought on by anxiety.

The bartender, drug pusher, occult practitioner, and other peddlers of
escapism all have one thing in common: They really don't care about the
consumer. They are out to make a profit. Even worse, when the temporary "cure" wears off, we have to return to the same world with the added
problem of hangovers and other negative consequences of fake healers.

Internally, we desperately need the peace of God: "Be anxious for
nothing, but in everything by prayer and supplication with thanksgiving let your requests be made known to God. And the peace of God,
which surpasses all comprehension, shall guard your hearts and your
minds in Christ Jesus" (Philippians 4:6-7). The awareness of a troubled
spirit should drive us to find the peace of God by turning to Him and
assuming our responsibility to think upon that which is true, honor-
able, and right (verse 8).

The Power of the Believer

You shall know the truth, and the truth shall make you free.

JOHN 8:32

When I was a boy on the farm, my dad, my brother, and I would visit our neighbor's farm to share produce and labor. The neighbor had a yappy little dog that scared the socks off me. When it came barking around the corner, my dad and brother stood their ground, but I ran. Guess who the dog chased! I escaped to the top of our pickup truck while the little dog yapped at me from the ground.

Everyone except me could see that the little dog had no power over me except what I gave it. Furthermore, it had no inherent power to throw me up on the pickup; it was my *belief* that put me up there. That dog controlled me by using my mind, my emotions, my will, and my muscles, all of which were motivated by fear. Finally, I gathered up my courage, jumped off the pickup, and kicked a small rock at the mutt. Lo and behold, it ran!

Satan is like that yappy little dog: deceiving people into fearing him more than God. His power is in the lie. He is the father of lies (John 8:44) who deceives the whole world (Revelation 12:9), and consequently the whole world is under the influence of the evil one (1 John 5:19). He can do nothing about your position in Christ, but if he can deceive you into believing his lies about you and God, you will spend a lot of time on top of the pickup truck! You don't have to outshout him or outmuscle him to be free of his influence. You just have to *outtruth* him. Believe, declare, and act upon the truth of God's Word, and you will thwart Satan's strategy.

I have learned from the Scriptures and my experience that *truth* is the liberating agent. The power of Satan is in the lie, and the power of the believer is in knowing the truth. We are to pursue truth, not power.

Your New Skipper

We are under obligation, not to the flesh, to live according to the flesh—for if you are living according to the flesh, you must die.
ROMANS 8:12-13

When I was in the Navy, we called the captain of our ship "the Old Man." Our Old Man was tough and crusty, and nobody liked him. He used to go out drinking with all his chiefs while belittling and harassing his junior officers and making life miserable for the rest of us. He was not a good example of a naval officer. So when our Old Man got transferred to another ship, we all rejoiced. It was a great day for our ship.

Then we got a new skipper—a new Old Man. The old Old Man no longer had any authority over us; he was gone—completely out of the picture. But I was trained under that Old Man. So how do you think I related to the new Old Man? At first I responded to him just like I had been conditioned to respond to the old skipper. I tiptoed around him expecting him to bite my head off. That's how I had lived for two years around my first skipper.

But as I got to know the new skipper I realized that he wasn't a crusty old tyrant like my old Old Man. He wasn't out to harass his crew; he was a good guy, really concerned about us. But I had been programmed for two years to react a certain way when I saw a captain's braids. I didn't need to react that way any longer, but it took several months to recondition myself to the new skipper.

You also once served under a cruel, self-serving skipper: your old sinful self with its sinful nature. The admiral of that fleet is Satan himself, the prince of darkness. But by God's grace you have been transferred into Christ's kingdom (Colossians 1:13). You now have a new skipper: your new self which is infused with the divine nature of Jesus Christ, your new admiral. As a child of God, a saint, you are no longer under the authority of your old Old Man. He is dead, buried, gone forever.

So why do you still react as if your old skipper were still in control of your behavior? We'll answer that question in the next devotion.

Your Life Apart from God

If by the Spirit you are putting to death the deeds of the body, you will
live. For all who are being led by the Spirit of God, these are sons of God.
ROMANS 8:13-14

Why do you still react as if your old self were still in control of
your behavior? Because all the means by which you learned to
live independently of God are still programmed into your memories,
and they constitute what the Bible calls "the flesh." The flesh is that tendency within each person to operate independently of God and to center interests on self. An unsaved person functions totally in the flesh
(Romans 8:7-8), worshiping and serving the creature rather than the
Creator (Romans 1:25). Such persons "live for themselves" (2 Corinthians 5:15), even though many of their activities may appear to be motivated by concern for others.

When you were born again, your old self died and your new self
came to life, and you were made a partaker of Christ's divine nature.
But flesh patterns remain. You brought to your Christian commitment
a fully conditioned mind-set and lifestyle developed apart from God
and centered on yourself. Since you were born physically alive but spiritually dead, you had neither the presence of God nor the knowledge
of God's ways. So you learned to live your life independently of God. It
is this learned independence that makes the flesh hostile toward God.

During the years you spent separated from God, your worldly experiences thoroughly programmed your brain with thought patterns, memory traces, responses, and habits which are alien to God. So even though
your old self is gone, your flesh remains in opposition to God as a preprogrammed propensity for sin, which is living independently of God.

Be aware that you no longer have to obey that preprogrammed bent
to live independently of God. You are a child of God, and you are free
to choose to live by the Spirit and "not carry out the desire of the flesh"
(Galatians 5:16).

Changing Your Behavior

Walk by the Spirit, and you will not carry out the desire of the flesh.

GALATIANS 5:16

A careful distinction must be made concerning your relationship to the flesh as a Christian. There is a difference in Scripture between being *in* the flesh and walking *according* to the flesh. As a Christian, you are no longer in the flesh. That phrase describes people who are still spiritually dead (Romans 8:8), those who live independently of God. Everything they do, whether morally good or bad, is in the flesh.

You are not in the flesh; you are in Christ. You are no longer independent of God; you have declared your dependence upon Him by placing faith in Christ. But even though you are not in the flesh, you may still choose to walk *according* to the flesh (Romans 8:12-13). You may still act independently of God by responding to the mind-set, patterns, and habits ingrained in you by the world you lived in. Paul rebuked the immature Corinthian Christians as "fleshly" because of their expressions of jealousy, strife, division, and misplaced identity (1 Corinthians 3:1-3). He listed the evidences of fleshly living in Galatians 5:19-2 1. Unbelievers can't help but live according to the flesh because they are totally in the flesh. But your old skipper is gone. You are no longer in the flesh and you no longer need to live according to its desires.

Getting rid of the old self was God's responsibility, but rendering the flesh and its deeds inoperative is our responsibility (Romans 8:12). God has changed your nature, but it's your responsibility to change your behavior by "putting to death the deeds of the body" (Romans 8:13). You will gain victory over the flesh by learning to condition your behavior after your new skipper, your new self which is infused with the nature of Christ, and learning to transform your old pattern for thinking and responding to your sin-trained flesh by renewing your mind (Romans 12:2).

Signs and Wonders

If anyone says to you, "Look, here is the Christ!" or "There he is!" do not believe it. For false christs and false prophets will arise and perform great signs and wonders, so as to lead astray, if possible, even the elect.

MATTHEW 24:23-25 ESV

"God also bore witness by signs and wonders and various miracles and by gifts of the Holy Spirit distributed according to his will" (Hebrews 2:4 ESV). Signs and wonders accompanied the apostles in the early church but seemed to diminish in frequency as the church matured, which is evident in the book of Acts. Their purpose was to show mercy to the sick and afflicted, but also to authenticate their message. So it should not surprise us that Satan would, by the same means, attempt to lend credibility to his messengers as the end draws near.

Every occurrence of the words *signs* and *wonders* in the New Testament, either each by itself or in conjunction with the other, is associated with a false messiah, a false prophet, and a false teacher when the context is referring to the end times. That certainly doesn't mean that God isn't working miracles today. Every aspect of our life in Christ is a miracle. But we dare not be arrogant and think that we couldn't be led astray. The need for spiritual discernment cannot be overstated.

The best way to detect the counterfeit is to know the real Messiah, who was sinless and did nothing for personal gain, social enhancement, or materialistic wealth.

Active Faith

*You have faith, and I have works; show me your faith without
the works, and I will show you my faith by my works.*
JAMES 2:18

When my son Karl was just a toddler, I would stand him up on
the table and call for him to jump from the table into my arms.
Did Karl believe I would catch him? Yes. How did I know he believed?
Because he jumped. Suppose he wouldn't jump. "Do you believe I will
catch you, Karl?" I might coax, and he may nod yes. But if he never
jumps, does he really believe I will catch him? No. Faith is active, not
passive. Faith takes a stand. Faith makes a move. Faith speaks up.

There are a lot of Christians who claim to have great faith in God
but are spiritually lethargic and don't do anything. Faith without action
is not faith; it's dead, meaningless (James 2:17-18)! If it isn't expressed, it
isn't faith. In order to believe God and His Word, we must do what He
says. If you don't do what He says, you don't really believe Him. Faith
and action are inseparable.

Sadly, one of the common pictures of the church today is of a group
of people with an assumed faith but little action. We're thankful that
our sins are forgiven and that Jesus is preparing a place in heaven for us,
but we're basically cowering in fear and defeat in the world, just hang-
ing on until the rapture. We treat the church as if it's a hospital. We get
together to compare wounds and hold each other's hands, yearning for
Jesus to come take us away.

The church is not a hospital; it's a military outpost under orders to
storm the gates of hell. Every believer is on active duty, called to take
part in fulfilling the Great Commission (Matthew 28:19-20). Thankfully the church has an infirmary where we can minister to the weak
and wounded, and that ministry is necessary. But our real purpose is
to be change agents in the world, taking a stand, living by faith, and
accomplishing something for God. You can say you believe God and
His Word. But if you are not actively involved in His plan, are you really
a mature believer?

Don't Be Defensive

To this you have been called, because Christ also suffered for you,
leaving you an example, so that you might follow his steps. He
committed no sin, neither was deceit found in his mouth. When he
was reviled, he did not revile in return; when he suffered, he did not
threaten, but continued entrusting himself to him who judges justly.

1 PETER 2:21-23 ESV

When people attack our character, the natural response is to be defensive. But the godly response is to not retaliate in kind. It's not hard to spot the character defects in others, but pointing them out is not our responsibility, and those who do are in the wrong. Trying to defend ourselves against the judgments of others will only inflame the problem. "A soft answer turns away wrath, but a harsh word stirs up anger" (Proverbs 15:1 ESV).

Let them have their say, and then ask, "What do you suggest I do?" No one cuts down another from a position of strength. They're reacting according to the flesh, and a fleshly response from us will only make matters worse. "Beloved, never avenge yourselves, but leave it to the wrath of God" (Romans 12:19 ESV). Let God convict them of their sin. In all likelihood they are hurting, and if we can refrain from reacting to their cutting remarks, we might have an opportunity to help them. "Do not be overcome by evil, but overcome evil with good" (verse 21 ESV).

Relationships

*Do nothing from selfish ambition or conceit, but in humility count
others more significant than yourselves. Let each of you look not
only to his own interests, but also to the interests of others. Have
this mind among yourselves, which is yours in Christ Jesus.*

PHILIPPIANS 2:3-5 ESV

The mother of the sons of Zebedee asked Jesus to place her two sons above all others in His kingdom (Matthew 20:20-21), which caused the other ten disciples to be indignant (verse 24). Jesus addressed the disciples saying, "You know that the rulers of the Gentiles lord it over them, and their great ones exercise authority over them. It shall not be so among you. But whoever would be great among you must be your servant, and whoever would be first among you must be your slave, even as the Son of Man came not to be served but to serve, and to give his life as a ransom for many" (verses 25-28 ESV). Rather than climb over one another to get to the top, we should become as servants or slaves in God's kingdom.

Ideally, there is no competition between us in the kingdom of God. He has a place and purpose for all His children. All are significant, and every member of the body of Christ willingly gives of their time, talent, and treasure to the glory of God. Everyone accepts themselves for who they are in Christ and how God created them. Everyone assumes responsibility for their own character and willingly loves others by assisting in meeting their needs and helping them reach their potential.

If we all committed ourselves to become like Christ, we would have that mind among us. Unfortunately, not everyone will, but *we* can, and it is not conditional on whether others do. Relationships break down when we attack another person's character, focus on our own needs, or compare ourselves with others. "When they measure themselves by one another and compare themselves with one another, they are without understanding" (2 Corinthians 10:12 ESV). We will never be fulfilled trying to be somebody other than ourselves. God accepts us for who we are. "Accept one another, just as Christ also accepted us to the glory of God" (Romans 15:7 NASB1995).

The Choice of Forgiveness

*Be kind to one another, tender-hearted, forgiving each
other, just as God in Christ has also forgiven you.*

EPHESIANS 4:32

Most of the ground that Satan gains in the lives of Christians is due to unforgiveness. We are warned to forgive others so that Satan cannot take advantage of us (2 Corinthians 2:10-11). God requires us to forgive others from our hearts or He will turn us over to the tormentors (Matthew 18:34-35). Why is forgiveness so critical to our freedom? Because of the cross. God didn't give us what we *deserve*; He gave us what we *needed* according to His mercy. We are to be merciful just as our heavenly Father is merciful (Luke 6:36). We are to forgive as we have been forgiven (Ephesians 4:31-32).

Forgiveness is not forgetting. People who try to forget find that they cannot. God says He will "remember no more" our sins (Hebrews 10:17), but God, being omniscient, cannot forget. "Remember no more" means that God will never use the past against us (Psalm 103:12). Forgetting may be a result of forgiveness, but it is never the means of forgiveness. When we bring up the past and use it against others, we haven't forgiven them.

Forgiveness is a choice, a crisis of the will. We choose to face and acknowledge the hurt and the hate in order to forgive from the heart. Since God requires us to forgive, it is something we can do. (He would never require us to do something we cannot do.) But forgiveness is difficult for us because it pulls against our concept of justice. We want revenge for offenses suffered. But we are told never to take our own revenge (Romans 12:19). "Why should I let them off the hook?" we protest. You let them off your hook, but they are never off God's hook. He will deal with them fairly—something we cannot do.

If you don't let offenders off your hook, you are hooked to them and the past, and that just means continued pain for you. Stop the pain; let it go. You don't forgive someone merely for their sake; you do it for your sake so you can be free. Your need to forgive isn't an issue between you and the offender; it's between you and God.

The Word in Our Hearts

Let the peace of Christ rule in your hearts, to which indeed you were called in one body. And be thankful. Let the word of Christ dwell in you richly.
COLOSSIANS 3:15-16 ESV

Imagine your mind is a coffeepot, filled with dark, smelly coffee. One day you decide to clean up your mind, but you have no way to filter out the coffee. Then you notice a bowl of crystal-clear ice beside the coffeepot with a label that says, "The Word of God." You can't pour the whole bowl in at once, but you can take one ice cube a day and fight off the temptation to put in another scoop of coffee.

Months later you can hardly smell, see, or taste the coffee that once filled the coffeepot. It's still there, but its influence is greatly diminished. However, there will be no progress if, as you put in one ice cube, you also put in one scoop of coffee (such as taking one peek at pornography or some other negative influence).

To rule literally means to act as an umpire, to arbitrate or decide. The peace of Christ should decide all matters of the heart for believers. "How can a young man keep his way pure? By guarding it according to your word. With my whole heart I seek you; let me not wander from your commandments! I have stored up your word in my heart, that I might not sin against you" (Psalm 119:9-11 ESV).

Scripture also reminds us, "The one who looks into the perfect law, the law of liberty, and perseveres, being no hearer who forgets but a doer who acts, he will be blessed in his doing" (James 1:25 ESV). The first application we make upon reading God's Word is to us. Allow the Holy Spirit to bring conviction and then correction for you to be trained in righteousness. God wants to enlarge the heart. "Search me, O God, and know my heart! Try me and know my thoughts! And see if there be any grievous way in me, and lead me in the way everlasting" (Psalm 139:23-24 ESV).

Called to Be a Saint

To those who have been sanctified in Christ Jesus, saints
by calling, with all who in every place call upon the name
of our Lord Jesus Christ, their Lord and ours.

1 Corinthians 1:2

Have you noticed that one of the most frequently used words of identity for Christians in the New Testament is saint? A saint is literally a holy person. Yet Paul and the other writers of the Epistles used the word generously to describe common, ordinary, everyday Christians like you and me. For example, Paul's salutation in 1 Corinthians 1:2 reads: "To the church of God which is at Corinth, to those who have been sanctified in Christ Jesus, saints by calling, with all who in every place call upon the name of our Lord Jesus Christ, their Lord and ours."

Notice that Paul didn't say that we are saints by hard work. He clearly states that we are saints by calling. Some of us have bought into the mentality that saints are people who have earned their lofty title by living a magnificent life or achieving a certain level of maturity. No way. The Bible says you are a saint because God called you to be a saint. You were "sanctified in Christ"—made a saint by participating in the life of the only true holy one, Jesus Christ.

Many Christians refer to themselves as sinners saved by grace. But are you really a sinner? Is that your scriptural identity? Not at all. God doesn't call you a sinner; He calls you a saint—a holy one. If you think of yourself as a sinner, guess what you will do: You'll live like a sinner; you'll sin. Why not identify yourself for who you really are: a saint who sins. Remember: What you do doesn't determine who you are; who you are determines what you do.

Since you are a saint in Christ by God's calling, you share in Christ's inheritance. That which is true of Christ is now true of you, because you are *in* Christ. It's part of your identity. You are not the great "I AM," but with Paul you can say, "By the grace of God I am what I am" (1 Corinthians 15:10).

Sowing and Reaping

Do not be deceived, God is not mocked; for whatever
a man sows, this he will also reap.

GALATIANS 6:7

The Scriptures are full of warnings about self-deception. James 1:26 reminds us that we deceive ourselves when we think we are religious but do not bridle our tongue. There is nothing that grieves God more than when we bad-mouth people instead of building them up with our speech. We are never to use our tongues to put others down. Instead we are to edify one another in what we say and thereby give grace to those who hear us. If your tongue is out of control, you're fooling yourself to believe that you have your spiritual life together.

We also deceive ourselves when we think we will not reap what we sow (Galatians 6:7). As Christians we sometimes think we are exempt from this principle, but we are not. Even though our sins are forgiven, we will have to live with the results and consequences of our thoughts, words, and actions, whether good or bad.

Since I was privileged to be raised on a farm, I witnessed every year the law of cause and effect. If we didn't sow good seed in the spring, we didn't reap a good crop in the fall. If we didn't feed the sheep, they died. Our young people have difficulty grasping this simple sow-and-reap truth. Living from weekend to weekend or party to party, they fail to prepare themselves for the future.

Your life may be measured by what you reap, but it is determined by what you sow. For example, if you want a friend, be a friend. What you get out of life is what you put into it.

Believing in Christ's Authority

*Truly I say to you, if you have faith as a mustard seed, you
shall say to this mountain, "Move from here to there," and
it shall move; and nothing shall be impossible to you.*

MATTHEW 17:20

What does it take to effectively exercise Christ's authority over spiritual powers? Can any Christian do so regardless of his level of spiritual maturity? If so, why aren't we more consistent in demonstrating our authority over Satan's kingdom?

I believe there are at least four qualifications for demonstrating authority over rulers and authorities in the spiritual realm. We'll consider them over the next few devotions.

The first qualification is *belief*. In the spiritual realm, if you don't believe you have authority, you're not going to exercise it. If your belief is weak, your expression of it will also be weak and ineffective. But if you grasp with confidence the authority that Christ has conferred upon you, you will exercise it with confidence.

Imagine a rookie traffic cop approaching a busy intersection to direct traffic for the first time. They told him at the academy that all he had to do was step into the street and hold up his hand and the cars would stop, but he's not so sure. He stands on the curb, tweets his whistle weakly, and sort of waves at an oncoming car, which roars by him. His authority is diminished by his lack of confidence.

Now imagine a seasoned officer coming on the scene. He sizes up the situation, steps into the street carefully but confidently, gives a blast on his whistle, and stretches out his hand—and the cars stop. There's no doubt in his mind that he's in control in that intersection because he has a settled belief in his authority.

You may consider yourself just a "rookie" at stopping the devil's traffic in your life. But Jesus Christ is a seasoned veteran, and you're in Him. Build your faith in your authority by studying how Jesus operated against the powers of darkness in the Gospels and how we are commanded to do so in the Epistles.

True Humility

Humble yourselves in the presence of the Lord, and He will exalt you.

JAMES 4:10

The second qualification for demonstrating authority over rulers and authorities in the spiritual realm is *humility*. Humility doesn't mean that you're always looking for a rock to crawl under because you feel unworthy to do anything. In exercising our authority, humility is placing confidence in Christ, the source of our authority, instead of in ourselves. Jesus didn't shrink back from exercising His authority, but He showed tremendous humility because He did everything according to what His Father told Him to do.

Pride says, "I resisted the devil all by myself." False humility says, "God resisted the devil; I did nothing." True humility says, "I resisted the devil by the grace of God." Apart from Christ we can do *nothing* (John 15:5), but that doesn't mean we're not supposed to do *something*. We exercise authority humbly in His strength and in His name.

Seeing humility as self-abasement is similar to seeing meekness as weakness. The Lord was meek, but He wasn't weak. Meekness is great strength under great control. Humility is confidence properly placed. We are to "glory in Christ Jesus and put no confidence in the flesh" (Philippians 3:3).

Pride is a killer. Pride says, "I can do it." No you can't. We absolutely need God, and we necessarily need each other.

Spirit-Inspired Boldness

Be strong and courageous! Do not tremble or be dismayed,
for the LORD your God is with you wherever you go.
JOSHUA 1:9

The third qualification for demonstrating authority over rulers and authorities in the spiritual realm is *boldness*. A Spirit-filled Christian is characterized by a true, godly sense of courage and boldness in spiritual warfare. On the eve of taking authority over the Promised Land, Joshua was challenged four times to be strong and courageous (Joshua 1:6, 7, 9, 18). When the early church prayed about their mission of sharing the gospel in Jerusalem, "the place where they had gathered together was shaken, and they were all filled with the Holy Spirit, and began to speak the word of God with boldness" (Acts 4:31). Spirit-inspired boldness is behind every successful advance in the church today.

The opposite of boldness is cowardice, fear, and unbelief. Notice what God thinks about these characteristics:

> I will give to the one who thirsts from the spring of the water of life without cost. He who overcomes shall inherit these things, and I will be his God and he will be My son. But for the cowardly and unbelieving and abominable and murderers and immoral persons and sorcerers and idolaters and all liars, their part will be in the lake that burns with fire and brimstone (Revelation 21:6-8).

That's pretty serious—cowards lined up at the lake of fire alongside murderers, sorcerers, and idolaters! It should serve to motivate us to exercise authority with boldness (2 Timothy 1:7).

A lot of Christians I meet fear the dark side of the spiritual world. It's true that a little knowledge can be a dangerous and frightful thing. But when we know who we are in Christ we have no reason to be afraid.

Dependence on God

I am the vine, you are the branches; he who abides in Me, and I in him, he bears much fruit; for apart from Me you can do nothing.

JOHN 15:5

The fourth qualification for demonstrating authority over rulers and authorities in the spiritual realm is *dependence*. A Spirit-filled life is dependent on God the Father. Even Jesus and the Holy Spirit modeled this dependency. Jesus said: "I can do nothing on My own initiative" (John 5:30); "Now they know that everything you have given me comes from you" (John 17:7 NIV); "But when He, the Spirit of truth, comes, He will guide you into all the truth; for He will not speak on His own initiative, but whatever He hears, He will speak" (John 16:13).

Spiritual authority is not an independent authority. We don't charge out on our own initiative like some kind of evangelical ghostbusters to hunt down the devil and engage him in combat. God's primary call is for each of us to focus on the ministry of the kingdom: loving, caring, preaching, teaching, praying, etc. However, when demonic powers challenge us in the course of pursuing this ministry, we deal with them on the basis of our authority in Christ and our dependence on Him. Then we carry on with our primary task.

Nor is the spiritual authority of the believer an authority to be exercised over other believers. We are to be "subject to one another in the fear of Christ" (Ephesians 5:21). There is a God-established authority on earth which governs the social structures of government, work, home, and church (Romans 13:1-7). It is critically important that we submit to these governing authorities unless they operate outside the scope of their authority, command us to do something against God's will, or restrict us from doing what God has commanded. Then we must obey God rather than people.

Unity in the Spirit

I therefore, a prisoner for the Lord, urge you to walk in a manner
worthy of the calling to which you have been called, with all humility
and gentleness, with patience, bearing with one another in love,
eager to maintain the unity of the Spirit in the bond of peace.

EPHESIANS 4:1-3 ESV

The unity of the Spirit is already present but not very evident. The only basis for unity among believers is to be united together in Christ. Believers are all children of God. Every attempt to unite fallen humanity on any other basis than Christ has failed.

The devil knows what we could accomplish if we were united together, so what is his strategy? First, he seeks to divide our minds because a double-minded person is unstable in all their ways. Second, Satan seeks to divide the family, because a house divided against itself cannot stand. In marriage, two become one in Christ. Third, he seeks to divide the body of Christ because divided we fall but united we stand. "There is one body and one Spirit...one Lord, one faith, one baptism, one God and Father of all, who is over all and through all and in all" (Ephesians 4:4-6 ESV).

In the High Priestly Prayer, Jesus asks that we be kept "from the evil one" (John 17:15 ESV), who seeks to divide our minds, marriages, and ministries. The Trinity is the perfect model of unity that Jesus prays will be the case for us: "[I ask] that they may all be one, just as you, Father, are in me, and I in you, that they also may be in us, so that the world may believe that you have sent me" (verses 20-21 ESV).

When believers resolve their personal and spiritual conflicts through genuine repentance and faith in God, there will be unity, and the peripheral things that once divided us will become incidental.

When Satan Targets Children

These words, which I am commanding you today, shall be on
your heart; and you shall teach them diligently to your sons.
DEUTERONOMY 6:6-7

Christian children and teenagers populating our schools, attending our churches, and living in our homes are the targets of Satan's strategy. Many Christian young people hear voices as if a subconscious self is talking to them. Satan seeks to destroy our families and churches by seducing our children away from their parents and from God (1 Timothy 4:1).

Is every evil thought in our mind the "voice" of Satan or a demon? No, the flesh—that part of our brain that urges us to operate independently of God and to center our interests on ourselves—also introduces sinful thoughts and suggests evil deeds. Furthermore, input from worldly movies, music, books, TV, etc. also introduces evil ideas into our minds. As we grow in Christ, we learn to say no to the deeds of the flesh and walk in the Spirit.

But the world and the flesh are not the only culprits, even though we tend to place most of the blame on them. The devil and "spiritual forces of wickedness" (Ephesians 6:12) are shrewdly at work introducing evil suggestions as thoughts or inner voices. Just as we learn to deal with worldly and fleshly influences, so we must learn to distinguish Satan's subtle, personal influence and resist him, and we must teach the next generations to do the same. Whether a child's evil thoughts are coming from the world, the flesh, or the devil, you need to help him bring "every thought captive to the obedience of Christ" (2 Corinthians 10:5).

Children aren't saying much about Satan's seduction in their lives because most of them don't know that he's at the heart of it. Satan is the great deceiver. He doesn't march into their lives accompanied by a brass band. He slyly worms his way in through the opportunities they and we give him. And when kids haven't been taught what the Bible says about Satan's strategies, they blame themselves, and their sense of guilt and fear of punishment further contributes to their silence.

One Fear-Object

It is the LORD of hosts whom you should regard as holy. And
He shall be your fear, and He shall be your dread.
ISAIAH 8:13

A severe storm hit, and the Coast Guard was summoned to respond to a ship in crisis. A new sailor proclaimed, "We can't go out. We'll never come back!" The seasoned captain responded, "We must go out. We don't have to come back." Duty called and responsibility overcame fear.

If we're going to walk by faith, there can be only one fear-object in our life, and that's God. We are responsible to Him. He is the ultimate fear-object because He is omnipotent and omnipresent. The fear of the Lord is healthy because it expels all other fears (Isaiah 8:11-14), which pale in comparison to our holy God. We need to be like David who said of Goliath, "Who is this uncircumcised Philistine, that he should taunt the armies of the living God?" (1 Samuel 17:26). The Hebrew army saw Goliath in relation to themselves and cowered in defeat. David saw Goliath in relation to God and conquered in His strength.

When the 12 spies checked out the Promised Land, ten said, "We are not able to go up against the people, for they are too strong" (Numbers 13:3 1). They didn't see God in the land, they saw giants (verse 33). With that perspective, "all the congregation lifted up their voices and cried, and the people wept" (Numbers 14:1).

Joshua and Caleb responded, "Do not rebel against the LORD; and do not fear the people of the land, for they shall be our prey. Their protection has been removed from them, and the LORD is with us; do not fear them" (Numbers 14:9). The people *did* rebel. They accepted the majority report instead of listening to Caleb and Joshua. By accepting the Canaanites' will over God's will, they elevated the power and eminence of the Canaanites over the omnipotence and omnipresence of God. To honor God as the ultimate fear-object is to worship Him. To be controlled by any other fear-object is to allow it to usurp God's place in our lives.

Our Defense Against Satan

The devil...does not stand in the truth, because there is no
truth in him. Whenever he speaks a lie, he speaks from his
own nature; for he is a liar, and the father of lies.
JOHN 8:44

Satan's power is in the lie. He has no power over you except what you give him when you believe his lies. You break his power when you expose the lie. Scripture says, "We know that we are of God, and the whole world lies in the power of the evil one" (1 John 5:19).

How much deception is actually going on in Christians today I can only speculate. In my ministry, I encounter it in nearly every counseling session. Many Christians I talk to struggle with oppressive thoughts, but they are afraid to tell anyone for fear that others will think they have a mental problem. Seldom do they realize that these distractions reflect the battle which is going on for their minds, even though Paul warned us: "The Spirit explicitly says that in latter times some will fall away from the faith, paying attention to deceitful spirits and doctrines of demons" (1 Timothy 4:1).

Since Satan's primary weapon is the lie, your defense against him is the truth. Dealing with Satan is not a power encounter; it's a truth encounter. When you expose Satan's lie with God's truth, his power is broken. That's why Jesus said: "You shall know the truth, and the truth shall make you free" (John 8:32). That's why He prayed: "My prayer is not that you take them out of the world but that you protect them from the evil one...Sanctify them by the truth; your word is truth" (John 17:15, 17 NIV). That's why the first piece of armor Paul mentions for standing against the schemes of the devil is the belt of truth (Ephesians 6:14). Satan's lie cannot withstand the truth any more than the darkness of night can withstand the light of the rising sun.

Wake-Up Call

Teacher, I beg you to look at my son, for he is my only child. And
behold, a spirit seizes him, and he suddenly cries out. It convulses him
so that he foams at the mouth, and shatters him, and will hardly leave
him. And I begged your disciples to cast it out, but they could not.
LUKE 9:38-40 ESV

Jesus called the 12 disciples, and they were to follow Him and observe Him do ministry. The next step in discipleship was to minister together, and the third step was for them to go out on their own while Jesus observed. The disciples had seen Jesus cast out demons and heal diseases, and now it was time for them to do kingdom ministry. They were to take nothing with them and rely only on their faith in God. "He called the twelve together and gave them power and authority over all demons and to cure diseases, and he sent them out to proclaim the kingdom of God and to heal" (Luke 9:1-2 ESV).

Sending out the Twelve was a learning experience for them because they had some kingdom-killing attitudes that needed correcting. In answer to the distraught father's request, Jesus said, "O faithless and twisted generation, how long am I to be with you and bear with you? Bring your son here." Then "while he was coming, the demon threw him to the ground and convulsed him. But Jesus rebuked the unclean spirit and healed the boy, and gave him back to his father. And all were astonished at the majesty of God" (Luke 9:41-43 ESV).

The two primary qualifications for kingdom work are belief and humility. If we doubt who we are in Christ and the authority we have over the enemy because of our position in Christ, we will likely retreat when the enemy threatens. On the other hand, Paul warned us not to think more highly of ourselves than we ought to think (Romans 12:3). "An argument arose among [the disciples] as to which of them was the greatest" (Luke 9:46 ESV), rendering them ineffective.

Relying on ourselves—or rituals, formulas, slogans, programs, or techniques—to set people free doesn't work. Only the truth and Jesus can set us free.

Under the Same Voice

*Come to Me, all who are weary and heavy-laden, and I will
give you rest. Take My yoke upon you, and learn from Me,
for I am gentle and humble in heart; and you shall find rest
for your souls. For My yoke is easy, and My load is light.*
MATTHEW 11:28-30

Matthew 11:28-30 contains a beautiful description of the purpose
and pace of the Spirit-filled walk. Jesus invites you to a restful
walk in tandem with Him, just as two oxen walk together under the
same yoke. "How can a yoke be restful?" you ask. Because Jesus' yoke
is an easy yoke. As the lead ox, Jesus walks at a steady pace. If you pace
yourself with Him, your burden will be easy. But if you take a passive
approach to the relationship, you'll be painfully dragged along in the
yoke because Jesus keeps walking. Or if you try to race ahead or turn
off in another direction, the yoke will chafe your neck and your life will
be uncomfortable. The key to a restful yoke-relationship with Jesus is
to learn from Him and open yourself to His gentleness and humility.

The picture of walking in the Spirit in tandem with Jesus also helps
us understand our service to God. How much will you get done without Jesus pulling on His side of the yoke? Nothing. And how much will
be accomplished without you on your side? Nothing. A yoke can only
work if both are pulling together.

Paul said, "I planted, Apollos watered, but God was causing the
growth" (1 Corinthians 3:6). You and I have the privilege to plant and
water, but if God isn't in it, nothing will grow. However, if we don't
plant and water, nothing will grow. God has chosen to work through
the church, in partnership with you to do His work in the world today.
He's the lead ox. Let's learn from Him.

Depression

How long, O LORD? Will you forget me forever? How long
will you hide your face from me? How long must I take
counsel in my soul and have sorrow in my heart all the
day? How long shall my enemy be exalted over me?
PSALM 13:1-2 ESV

Depression has been called the common cold of mental illness. When experiencing the "blues," we feel hopeless and helpless in the midst of our circumstances, and such was the case for David in Psalm 13. In Psalm 38, David expresses almost every symptom of depression (poor health—verse 3, despair—verse 4, mourning—verse 6, feebleness—verse 8, low energy—verse 10, being isolated and withdrawn—verse 11, negative thoughts—verse 12). God sought out David because he was "a man after his own heart" (1 Samuel 13:14 ESV).

In Psalm 13, however, David is depressed for one major reason: He thinks God has forgotten him forever. God couldn't forget anyone even for a moment much less forever. But if that is what we believe, then we feel helpless and hopeless. David overcomes depression by first recalling, "I have trusted in your steadfast love" (verse 5 ESV). Then he expresses hope: "My heart shall rejoice in your salvation" (verse 5 ESV). Finally, he exercises his will: "I will sing to the LORD" (verse 6 ESV).

Jeremiah has been called the "weeping prophet," and he's the likely author of Lamentations. In chapter 3, he believes God is the cause of his afflictions, and he feels bitter and depressed. He believes God is the source of his problems and that He "walled" him in. Jeremiah was mired in depression and ready to call it quits until he thought, "But this I call to mind, and therefore I have hope: The steadfast love of the LORD never ceases; his mercies never come to an end; they are new every morning; great is your faithfulness. 'The LORD is my portion,' says my soul, 'therefore I will hope in him'" (verses 21-24 ESV).

Martin Luther, like David, had numerous bouts with depression, and like David, he turned to music to overcome his sorrow. We are the benefactors. He wrote "A Mighty Fortress Is Our God."

Trusting Children

I rejoice that in everything I have confidence in you.
2 CORINTHIANS 7:16

When I was 14 years old my family moved off the farm in Minnesota where I was born. But I never adjusted to our new home in Arizona. When I was only 15 my parents let me take a bus back to Minnesota to work on the farm for the summer. The following summer I drove an old car back to Minnesota by myself. The family I stayed with asked if I would like to live with them and finish high school in Minnesota. To my great joy my parents said it was okay.

What impact did my parents' trust have on me? I never wanted to do anything to lose their trust. Their trust in me was a great driving force in my life and the greatest gift they ever gave me. Next to the Holy Spirit in me, that trust has been the greatest deterrent to immorality. Even years later when I was in the military and thousands of miles from home, I didn't want to lose their trust.

When you effectively communicate your love, trust, and respect to your children (or to children under your care), they will learn to value these qualities so much that they will never intentionally do anything to lose them. Then when they are introduced to Christ, they will also value His love, trust, and respect. "But my child isn't trustworthy," you say. Neither are you completely trustworthy. Yet God has entrusted you with the gospel. That gives you something to live up to. What can you possibly gain by communicating anything less than your trust in a child?

Paul wrote to the church at Corinth: "I rejoice that in everything I have confidence in you" (2 Corinthians 7:16). But Corinth was a messed up place. Is Paul's statement a bunch of psychological hype? No, I don't think so. Paul's confidence was in the Lord, and he knew that the work God had begun in the Corinthian believers would be completed. Under the inspiration of God he also knew that expressing belief and confidence in them was foundational for building them up.

What We Treasure

Do not lay up for yourselves treasures upon earth, where moth and rust destroy, and where thieves break in and steal. But lay up for yourselves treasures in heaven.
MATTHEW 6:19-20

There are material goods which Jesus identifies as "treasures upon earth." And there are immaterial goods which Jesus calls "treasures in heaven." Treasures upon earth have two characteristics.

First, all natural things decay. What rust doesn't destroy, moths or termites will. Second, because of the value of earthly treasures, there is always a concern for security. It is hard to be anxiety-free if we are worried about our possessions. The more we possess, the more we cause others to covet, hence the reason why "thieves break in and steal."

On the other hand, treasures in heaven are beyond the reach of thieves and secure from the ravages of moths and rust. Paul puts it this way: "Discipline yourself for the purpose of godliness; for bodily discipline is only of little profit, but godliness is profitable for all things, since it holds promise for the present life and also for the life to come" (1 Timothy 4:7-8).

What do you treasure in your heart? What would you exchange for love, joy, peace, patience, kindness, goodness, faithfulness, gentleness, and self-control? Would you exchange these qualities for a new car, a cabin in the hills, a boat in the marina, exceptional status at the top of the corporate ladder?

Achievement is determined by who or what you serve. There is a moral healthiness and simple, unaffected goodness present in the single-minded person that is absent from the one serving many masters. Jesus said, "No one can serve two masters; for either he will hate the one and love the other, or he will hold to one and despise the other. You cannot serve God and mammon. For this reason I say to you, do not be anxious" (Matthew 6:24-25).

There will be no peace serving two masters. To whichever master we yield, by that master we shall be controlled.

Fences Around the Laws

You are not under law, but under grace.
ROMANS 6:14

In His ministry, Jesus often violated the traditional instructions surrounding the observance of the Sabbath because they were a clear distortion of God's commandment. A common practice, born out of a desire to protect a known law or principle, is to establish additional rules to keep us from breaking the laws or violating the principles. We establish fences around the laws, but within a short time the fences become laws.

For instance, we are not to be unequally yoked (2 Corinthians 6:14-15). To ensure that this doesn't happen, we sometimes build a fence around the law by establishing additional rules such as, "You can't associate with or date a non-Christian." That may be advisable in some cases, but don't make it a law. Some have gone to the extreme by requiring that their children never associate with non-Christians. This makes the Great Commission a formidable task!

Here's another example. A common practice in many churches, left over from the Prohibition era, is to require total abstinence from alcohol. Again, that may be wise in many cases, but the Bible instructs against strong drink and drunkenness and teaches us to do all things in moderation. The major biblical concern is not the alcohol, but whether we're being a stumbling block to a weaker brother. Total abstinence may actually keep some from the medicine they need or it may be detrimental when relating to a weaker brother.

The point is, we can easily distort the true Word of God by adding our own traditional practices and making them equal with the original intent of God. We may need to stand against pharisaic practices as the Lord did—before we find ourselves in bondage to man-made traditions.

Taming the Tongue

Let no corrupting talk come out of your mouths, but only such
as is good for building up, as fits the occasion, that it may give
grace to those who hear. And do not grieve the Holy Spirit of
God, by whom you were sealed for the day of redemption.
EPHESIANS 4:29-30 ESV

Many of the problems in our churches and homes would disappear overnight if we obeyed the above command. It grieves God when we use our tongues to tear down one another instead of building up one another. James said, "The tongue is set among our members, staining the whole body, setting on fire the entire course of life, and set on fire by hell" (James 3:6 ESV). Chrysostom said, "If you let it run wild, it becomes the vehicle of the devil and his angels."[1] James adds, "No human being can tame the tongue" (verse 8 ESV), but God can.

"Out of the abundance of the heart the mouth speaks. The good person out of his good treasure brings forth good" (Matthew 12:34-35 ESV). A heart fully devoted to God speaks grace to those who hear. "But if you have bitter jealousy and selfish ambition in your hearts, do not boast and be false to truth. This is not the wisdom that comes down from above, but is earthly, unspiritual, demonic" (James 3:14-15 ESV). For example, God tells us that the worst of the false prophets are those who leverage people by saying, "declares the LORD" (Jeremiah 23:31 ESV). They are implying that we would be disobeying God if we didn't pay attention to them. Tragic marriages have come about when people have said, "The Lord told me we're to get married." Pulling rank by using God's name or claiming special insight into His Word is manipulative.

Whether we are a spokesperson for God or a spokesperson for the enemy is determined by choice and the condition of our hearts.

Spiritual Discernment

*Give your servant a discerning heart to govern your people
and to distinguish between right and wrong.*
1 KINGS 3:9 NIV

Discernment is an overlooked spiritual discipline in many churches. But in reality, spiritual discernment should be our first line of defense against deception. It's that "buzzer" inside, warning you that something is wrong. For example, you visit someone's home and everything appears in order. But you can cut the air with a knife. Even though nothing visible confirms it, your spirit detects that something is wrong in that home.

The first step to understanding discernment is to understand the motive which is essential for employing it. In 1 Kings 3:9, Israel's king Solomon cries out to God for help. God answers:

"Because you have asked this thing and have not asked for yourself long life, nor have asked riches for yourself, nor have you asked for the life of your enemies, but have asked for yourself discernment to understand justice, behold, I have done according to your words. Behold, I have given you a wise and discerning heart" (verses 11-12). The motive for true discernment is never to promote self, to amass personal gain, or to secure an advantage over another person—even an enemy.

The Greek word for *discernment—diakrino*—simply means to make a judgment or a distinction. Discernment has one primary function: to distinguish right from wrong. In 1 Corinthians 12:10 discernment is the divinely enabled ability to distinguish a good spirit from a bad spirit.

Discernment is not a function of the mind; it's a function of the Holy Spirit which is in union with your soul/spirit. When the Spirit sounds a warning, your mind may not be able to perceive what's wrong. Have the courage to acknowledge that something is wrong when your spirit is troubled. Share what you are sensing with others, and ask the Lord for wisdom.

Faith Leads to Understanding

Make every effort to supplement your faith with virtue, and virtue with knowledge, and knowledge with self-control...
2 Peter 1:5-6 esv

Supplementing our faith with virtue and then knowledge would seem to be out of order, but it wasn't so throughout most of church history. The church fathers understood that faith led to understanding. The Enlightenment precipitated a reverse in that order, thinking that understanding would lead to faith. The historical doctrines of the church that failed to meet the standard of human reason were questioned. So it's not surprising that the incarnation, the resurrection, and the Trinity were discarded by liberal philosophers. What they couldn't humanly understand, they didn't believe.

What they really didn't comprehend is that "the foolishness of God is wiser than men" (1 Corinthians 1:25 esv). We're confronted every day with the choice to either exalt ourselves or humble ourselves before Almighty God. "We know that 'all of us possess knowledge.' This 'knowledge' puffs up, but love builds up. If anyone imagines that he knows something, he does not yet know as he ought to know. But if anyone loves God, he is known by God" (8:1-3 esv).

When we choose to put our faith in God, our eyes are opened and we begin to understand. "Oh, the depth of the riches and wisdom and knowledge of God! How unsearchable are his judgments and how inscrutable his ways!" (Romans 11:33 esv). The finite can never fully understand the infinite. "For as the heavens are higher than the earth, so are my ways higher than your ways and my thoughts than your thoughts" (Isaiah 55:9 esv).

Living a virtuous life may seem to be keeping us from the pleasures of this world, but those who do will understand the value of moral purity and faithfulness later in life.

Significance

Make every effort to supplement your faith with virtue, and virtue
with knowledge, and knowledge with self-control, and self-control
with steadfastness, and steadfastness with godliness, and godliness
with brotherly affection, and brotherly affection with love. For if
these qualities are yours and are increasing, they keep you from being
ineffective or unfruitful in the knowledge of our Lord Jesus Christ.
2 PETER 1:5-8 ESV

Peter lays out a clear path for significance on which any believer can embark. No spiritual gifts, or talents, or titles, or ecclesiastical positions are mentioned. It's all about becoming the person God created us to be. Godly character is what qualifies us for spiritual leadership. Jesus said, "By this all people will know that you are my disciples, if you have love for one another" (John 13:35 ESV). Love is the highest attainment on Peter's list and the goal of our instruction according to Paul (1 Timothy 1:5 ESV).

But what if we're searching for significance on another path? Or stagnant in our growth? "Whoever lacks these qualities is so nearsighted that he is blind, having forgotten that he was cleansed from his former sins" (2 Peter 1:9 ESV). In other words, we have forgotten that we are children of God. If that is our case, what should we do? "Therefore, brothers, be all the more diligent to confirm your calling and election, for if you practice these qualities you will never fall" (verse 10 ESV). What a promise!

The Total Realm of Reality

Seek first His kingdom and His righteousness; and
all these things shall be added to you.
Matthew 6:33

A common question I am asked by those who believe the Bible and accept the reality of the spiritual world is, "When is a problem spiritual and when is it psychological or neurological?" Our problems are never not psychological. Our mind, will, and emotions, along with developmental matters, always contribute something to the problem and are necessary for the resolution. At the same time, our problems are never not spiritual. God is always present. Furthermore, it is never safe to take off the armor of God. The possibility of being deceived, tempted, and accused by Satan is a continuous reality.

Our culture assumes that any problem related to the mind must be psychological or neurological. Why can it not be spiritual? We must take into account the total realm of reality: body, soul, and spirit. If we don't, we will polarize into a psychotherapeutic ministry that ignores spiritual reality or some kind of deliverance ministry that ignores developmental matters or human responsibility. The diagnosis and resolution of our problems must take into account both the psychological and the spiritual. I have assured hundreds of people under spiritual attack that they are not going crazy but that there is a battle going on for their minds. The relief this insight brings to people is incredible.

I fully acknowledge that some problems are caused by chemical imbalances or glandular disorders. For these you had better see your family physician. But it seems that the last possibility to be considered is always the spiritual, and only after every other possible natural explanation has been exhausted. But since we are instructed to seek first the kingdom of God, why not check out the spiritual area first? Frankly, I approach every problem hoping it is spiritual in nature, because I know on the authority of the Word of God that the problem is resolvable. If the battle is for the mind, we can win that war.

Doing God's Work

The LORD will continually guide you.
ISAIAH 58:11

An important concept of God's will is that God can only guide a moving ship. He is the rudder, but if the ship isn't under way it can't be directed. Willingness to obey His will gets the ship moving.

In Acts 15:36, Paul had decided to revisit the churches he helped establish on his first missionary trip. The churches were being strengthened and increasing in number (Acts 16:5). Luke reports:

> And they passed through the Phrygian and Galatian region, having been forbidden by the Holy Spirit to speak the word in Asia; and when they had come to Mysia, they were trying to go into Bithynia, and the Spirit of Jesus did not permit them; and passing by Mysia, they came down to Troas. And a vision appeared to Paul in the night: a certain man of Macedonia was standing and appealing to him, and saying, "Come over to Macedonia and help us" (Acts 16:6-9).

Sometimes God's leading does not make sense. If God wanted Paul to go to Macedonia in the first place, why didn't He make it easier and faster by having Paul travel by land to Caesarea and sail to Macedonia? Because God starts us out on a life course to fulfill a certain purpose and then, only when we are ready, He gives us course corrections. Like a good river pilot, He steers us away from troubled waters, and like a good coach, He never puts us in the game until we are ready.

I believe in divine guidance as described in Isaiah 58:11. But the context reveals that there are prerequisites that have to be satisfied. We are sometimes like a person who seeks to be an athlete by simply suiting up for the race. That's not how the skills are gained. It's in the course of dedication, training, and the contest itself that one gains the skill of an athlete.

It's in the doing of God's work that His will becomes known.

Stress

Preparing your minds for action, and being sober-minded,
set your hope fully on the grace that will be brought
to you at the revelation of Jesus Christ.
1 PETER 1:13 ESV

Our adrenal glands respond when we're under a certain amount of stress by secreting cortisol (a natural hormone) into our bloodstream. This is a natural flight or fight response to the pressures of life. When stress persists too long, it becomes distress, the system breaks down, and we become physically sick. Stress is a major cause of heart disease and cancer.

However, when two people of equal stature are subjected to the same environment, one can flourish while the other doesn't. The difference is how they perceive the environment—in other words, what they believe about what they're experiencing. We are not shaped by our environment; we are shaped by how we perceive it. Our five senses bring data to the brain, but the mind interprets it. That is what determines the signal sent to our adrenal glands.

We have no control of our glands, which are part of the autonomic nervous system, but we do have control of what we think and believe. Rather than being controlled by outside circumstances, believers should be directed from within. Jesus was never stressed out, and we have the same potential if we are sober-minded, because "we have the mind of Christ" (1 Corinthians 2:16 ESV). Wisdom is seeing life from God's perspective.

Mental Constructs

One thing I do: forgetting what lies behind and straining forward to what lies ahead, I press on toward the goal for the prize of the upward call of God in Christ Jesus.
PHILIPPIANS 3:13-14

Paul lost everything he had when God struck him down. He lost all his Jewish friends, his reputation, his social status, and his self-respect, and he had to live with the fact that he was the chief of all sinners, having zealously persecuted the church. After his conversion, he went away for three years. Undoubtedly, this was to renew his mind, but it's safe to assume that this was also a time to grieve over his losses, overcome his disappointments, and rebuild a shattered perception of himself.

It took some time for Paul to bounce back after his losses, but some people never recover. Three mental constructs determine how long it will take, if ever, to recover from tragedies. The first is whether we think the consequences have a short- or long-term effect on us. Depression will be prolonged if we believe a loss will have a negative impact for the rest of our lives.

The second is how pervasive we believe the negative consequences are. If we believe they will ruin our whole lives, they just may. We grieve over losses, but a prolonged depression signifies an overattachment to people, places, and things that we have no right or ability to control.

The third is when we overly personalize the crisis and believe it's all our fault.

To overcome our losses, we need to change how we think from *I'm the problem* to *It's a problem*. From *In everything* to *In this one thing*. From *Forever* to *For a season*. Someone said, "The bend in the road is not the end of the road, unless we fail to make the turn." Paul made the turn and then pressed on to become a model of perseverance and devotion to Christ.

Already Accepted

*If we walk in the light as He Himself is in the light, we have fellowship
with one another, and the blood of Jesus His Son cleanses us from all sin.*
1 JOHN 1:7

Fellowship with God is not an abstract theological concept but a living relationship. Living in continuous agreement with God is to walk in the light. Satan can't accuse me if I live in the light, but walking in the light is not moral perfection (1 John 1:8). We are not sinless, but the confession mentioned in 1 John 1:9 brings us into agreement with God about our present moral condition before Him.

What makes it possible to be this open with God about our condition is the fact that we are already His children. Our eternal state is not at stake, only our daily victory. We don't have to pretend with God in the hope that He will accept us. As His children we're already accepted, so we are free to be honest with Him. We have no relationship to lose, only fellowship to gain. Knowing that we're secure in Christ, we can express ourselves honestly to Him. He already knows the thoughts and intentions of our hearts (Hebrews 4:12).

Knowing that we are forgiven, let's come before His presence with thanksgiving. God is our Father, and like any parent He doesn't appreciate grumbling, complaining children, especially since this Father sacrificed His only begotten Son for us. He will not be very interested in our list of demands if we haven't been obedient to Him. I also don't think He is going to be very interested in helping us develop our own kingdoms when we are to work at establishing the only one that will last—His!

To sit in the presence of my Father who loves me, who has made an incredible sacrifice so I can be there, doesn't have to be a dismal, failing experience. He invites us into His presence just as we are, because in Christ our weakness and sin have been covered: "Let us draw near with a sincere heart in full assurance of faith, having our hearts sprinkled clean from an evil conscience" (Hebrews 10:22).

Clean House

Put to death therefore what is earthly in you: sexual immorality, impurity,
passion, evil desire, and covetousness, which is idolatry. On account of
these the wrath of God is coming. In these you too once walked, when
you were living in them. But now you must put them all away.

COLOSSIANS 3:5-8 ESV

O ur bodies are like houses that need to be regularly cleaned. We are
going to attract a lot of flies if we don't take out the garbage. One
person calls the Power Exterminating Service. They study the flight patterns of the flies, try to determine their names and rank, and then cast
them out. Those flies find seven other flies and tell them where the garbage is.

A second person calls the Negotiating Exterminating Service. They
enter into a dialogue with the flies, trying to extract information from
them, seemingly unaware that they're all liars. While they're talking to
the flies, the owner blanks out and lets the exterminator assume responsibility for him.

A third person calls the Heavenly House Cleaning Service. They
ignore the flies and talk to the owner. Together they clean out all the
garbage that has attracted the flies, fill the place with the Holy Spirit,
causing the flies to flee, and then they seal off all entry points.

Repentance and faith in God have been the means to resolve personal and spiritual conflicts and will continue to be the answer throughout this church age.

God Gently Guides

And your ears will hear a word behind you, "This is the way,
walk in it," whenever you turn to the right or to the left.
ISAIAH 30:21

In a telephone conversation a lady asked, "Dr. Anderson, my pastor says my favorite television evangelist is a false teacher. Is he right?"

At a ministerial retreat, a pastor stopped me and said, "Neil, I've been at this church three years, and here's the situation…" After finishing his description, he asked, "Do you think God is calling me out of there?"

A seminary student stopped by my office and asked, "You've met with my girlfriend and me twice now. Do you think we should get married?"

Good questions. Important questions for those asking them. They all hinge on the answer to a much larger question: Does God communicate His will to us? If so, how?

Each of these fine Christians was looking for direction or confirmation of God's leading. Possibly they lacked the spiritual discernment to make the right decision. They were thinking that I, like the referee in a game, would make the right "call" for them. I can advise and share what I know Scripture teaches, but only God can give divine guidance.

You can know God's will for your life. Ephesians 5:17 instructs us, "Do not be foolish, but understand what the will of the Lord is." God doesn't instruct us to do something we cannot do. The will of God is knowable. In the first place, we have the Bible, God's Word, which the Holy Spirit will enlighten for us as we meditate on it, providing us with remarkably clear guidance in most areas of our life. Second, we usually can experience the direct guidance of the Holy Spirit in areas not specifically covered by God's Word—if we are spiritually free and desire to do His will.

I have come to deeply believe that God gently guides our steps as we choose to walk with Him. I believe in divine guidance. I believe that God wants to make His presence known in our lives and in our ministries.

Following our Shepherd

For all who are being led by the Spirit of God, these are sons of God.

ROMANS 8:14

I had the privilege of feeding and caring for the sheep on the farm where I was raised. I discovered that sheep aren't the smartest animals on the farm. Sheep need to be shepherded. Left to themselves in a lush pasture, they will keep eating until it kills them. They need a shepherd to make them "lie down in green pastures" (Psalm 23:2) so they don't eat themselves to death!

The Lord often pictured our relationship with Him in Scripture like that of a shepherd and his sheep. Those of us who live in the West don't have a correct picture of what it means to be led like sheep. Western shepherds drive their sheep from behind the flock, often using dogs to bark at their heels. Eastern shepherds, like those in Bible times, lead their sheep from in front. I watched a shepherd lead his flock on a hillside outside Bethlehem during a visit to the Holy Land. The shepherd sat on a rock while the sheep grazed. After a time he stood up, said a few words to the sheep, and walked away. The sheep looked up and followed him. It was fascinating! The words of Jesus in John 10:27 suddenly took on new meaning to me: "My sheep hear My voice, and I know them, and they follow Me."

Sheep without a shepherd become disoriented and scatter. Rams arise from the flock and butt heads to determine who will lead. The ones with the hardest heads win. Without a shepherd, we too are left to the mercy of hard-headed, driven people or we wander around directionless, eating ourselves to death.

The Spirit-walk is one of being led, not driven. God won't make you walk in the Spirit, and the devil can't make you walk in the flesh, although he will certainly try to draw you in that direction. You are free to choose to follow the leading of the Spirit or the desires of the flesh (Romans 8:14).

High Priestly Prayer

*I have given them your word, and the world has hated them because
they are not of the world, just as I am not of the world. I do not ask
that you take them out of the world, but that you keep them from
the evil one...Sanctify them in the truth; your word is truth. As
you sent me into the world, so I have sent them into the world.*

JOHN 17:14-15, 17-18 ESV

Given the present state of this fallen world, have you ever wondered
what God's perspective is? What would be His first concern? I
believe we are given that perspective in the High Priestly Prayer.

Jesus was about to return to heaven and leave behind the Eleven. (He
had already lost Judas, who was deceived by Satan.) His first concern was
that we be kept from the evil one, and the answer is to be sanctified in
truth. The church of the living God is the "pillar and buttress of truth"
(1 Timothy 3:15 ESV). Without the truth, we would never know the
love of God. Without the love of God, we would never know the truth.

Jesus said, "I do not ask for these only, but also for those who believe
in me through their word, that they may all be one" (John 17:20-21 ESV).
United we stand, but divided we fall. Finally, Jesus asked "that the love
with which you have loved me may be in them, and I in them" (verse
26 ESV). The church will be protected and triumphant if we stay committed to the truth, work together in unity, and are known for our love.

Maintaining Your Freedom

*It was for freedom that Christ set us free; therefore keep standing
firm and do not be subject again to a yoke of slavery.*

GALATIANS 5:1

The Revolutionary War was a hard-fought battle, and many lives
were lost in order to ensure the freedom of our country. There is
always a price to pay for freedom, and the moment we take our freedom for granted, we run the risk of losing it.

Freedom in Christ from our sinful nature and the god of this world
is the inheritance of every believer. Christ has set you free through His
victory over sin and death on the cross. But if you have lost a measure
of your freedom because you have failed to stand firm in the faith or
you have disobeyed God, it is your responsibility to do whatever is necessary to maintain a right relationship with God. Your eternal destiny
is not at stake; you are secure in Christ. But your daily victory in Him
will be tenuous at best if you fail to assume your responsibility to maintain your freedom in Christ.

Remember: You are not the helpless victim of a tug-of-war between
two nearly equal heavenly superpowers. Compared to Satan's limited
attributes, God is immeasurable in His omnipotence, omnipresence,
and omniscience—and you are united with Him! Sometimes the reality
of sin and the presence of evil may seem more real than the reality and
presence of God, but that's part of Satan's deception. He is a defeated foe,
and we are in Christ the eternal Victor. That's why we worship God: to
keep His divine attributes constantly before us in order to counter Satan's
lies. A true knowledge of God and our identity in Christ is the greatest
determinant of our mental health. A false concept of God and the misplaced deification of Satan are the greatest contributors to mental illness.

Are you walking in freedom today?

Dead to Sin

You also must consider yourselves dead to sin
and alive to God in Christ Jesus.
ROMANS 6:11 ESV

We are to consider true for us what is true of Jesus Christ's relationship with sin and death. This is not made true by experience, nor is it a command to be obeyed. It is a blessed spiritual fact to be believed. Paul now shifts from the past tense (indicative) concerning what Christ has done, to the present tense (imperative), instructing what we must do to live a righteous life. We must consider ourselves dead to sin, but that isn't what makes us dead to sin. We consider it so because it is so. We are to believe we are no longer under the dominion of sin.

Sin is still powerful and appealing, and we can commit sin, not as slaves but as those who are under the dominion of sin. But when it knocks on our door, we don't have to answer. "Sin will have no dominion over you, since you are not under law but under grace" (Romans 6:14 ESV).

"Let not sin therefore reign in your mortal body, to make you obey its passions. Do not present your members to sin as instruments for unrighteousness, but present yourselves to God as those who have been brought from death to life, and your members to God as instruments for righteousness" (Romans 6:12-13 ESV).

It's our responsibility to not allow sin to reign in our mortal bodies, and we do that by not using them as instruments of unrighteousness. Notice that this passage has one negative and two positive instructions. Since we belong to God, we can present or dedicate ourselves only to God, but we can use our bodies as instruments of righteousness or unrighteousness. Our bodies can be used for good or evil.

If we wake up in the morning feeling alive to sin and dead to Christ, and we believe what we feel, we will have a bad day. We will have a better day if we awake and say, *"I'm alive in Christ and dead to sin. Thank You, Jesus."*

Our Greatest Motivation

The fear of the LORD is the beginning of knowledge;
fools despise wisdom and instruction.

PROVERBS 1:7

To worship God is to acknowledge His divine attributes. He doesn't need us to tell Him who He is. We need to keep our minds renewed to the reality of His presence. Notice how this is brought out in 2 Corinthians 5:9-11: "Therefore also we have as our ambition, whether at home or absent, to be pleasing to Him. For we must all appear before the judgment seat of Christ, that each one may be recompensed for his deeds in the body, according to what he has done, whether good or bad. Therefore knowing the fear of the Lord, we persuade men."

Realizing that God knows the thoughts and intentions of our hearts, we should be motivated to live our lives to please Him. Someday we're going to stand before Him and give an account. The judgment that Paul is talking about in this passage is not for punishment but for rewards. We don't fear God because of the possibility of punishment: "There is no fear in love; but perfect love casts out fear, because fear involves punishment, and the one who fears is not perfected in love" (1 John 4:18). We have already been judged as to *where* we will spend eternity. But *how* we spend eternity depends on how we respond to God in this lifetime.

I personally don't want to limp into heaven and have Him say, "Well, okay, come on in." I want to stand before God someday and hear Him say, "Well done, good and faithful servant. Enter into the joy of your Lord." That's the greatest motivation in my life. As a child I didn't fear the spanking of my father nearly as much as I feared being accountable to him and facing his disappointment.

I'm not disappointed with God, and I sure don't want Him disappointed with me.

Every Christian's Responsibility

*Humble yourselves, therefore, under the mighty hand of
God, that He may exalt you at the proper time, casting all
your anxiety upon Him, because He cares for you.*

1 Peter 5:6-7

Several weeks after one of my conferences, a friend shared with me the story of a dear Christian woman who had attended. She had lived in deep depression for several years. She "survived" by leaning on her friends, three counseling sessions a week, and a variety of prescription drugs.

During the conference, this woman realized that her support system included everybody and everything but God. She had not cast her anxiety on Christ and she was anything but dependent on Him. She took her conference syllabus home and began focusing on her identity in Christ and expressing confidence in Him to meet her daily needs. She radically threw off all her other supports (a practice I do not recommend) and decided to trust in Christ alone to relieve her depression. She began living by faith in God rather than mankind and renewing her mind according to Scripture. After only one month she was a completely different person. The support of a caring community can become a poor substitute for our own personal relationship with God.

Persons who want to move forward in Christian maturity can certainly benefit from the discipling of others. And those who seek freedom from their past can be helped through the counseling of others. But ultimately every Christian is responsible for his or her own maturity and freedom in Christ. Nobody can make you grow. That's your decision and daily responsibility. We absolutely need God, and we also need the support of one another. Thankfully, none of us walks through the disciplines of personal maturity and freedom alone. The indwelling Christ is eagerly willing to walk with us each step of the way.

The Source of All Hope

Hope in God, for I shall again praise Him, the
help of my countenance, and my God.
PSALM 43:5

Sometimes the depression resulting from a seemingly impossible situation is related to a wrong concept of God. David wrote: "How long, O Lord? Will you forget me forever? How long will you hide your face from me?...How long will my enemy triumph over me?" (Psalm 13:1-2 NIV). Had God really forgotten David? Was He actually hiding from David? Of course not. David had a wrong concept of God, feeling that He had abandoned him to the enemy. David believed a lie about God, and consequently he lost his focus. His situation seemed hopeless, and hopelessness is the basis for all depression.

But the remarkable thing about David is that he didn't stay in the dumps. He evaluated his situation and realized, *Hey, I'm a child of God. I'm going to focus on what I know about Him, not on my negative feelings.* From the pit of his depression he wrote: "I trust in your unfailing love; my heart rejoices in your salvation" (Psalm 13:5 NIV). Then he decided to make a positive expression of his will: "I will sing the LORD's praise, for he has been good to me" (verse 6 NIV). He willfully moved away from his wrong concept and its accompanying depression and returned to the source of his hope.

If Satan can destroy your belief in God, you will lose your source of hope. But with God all things are possible. He is the source of all hope. You need to learn to respond to hopeless-appearing situations as David did: "Why are you in despair, O my soul? And why are you disturbed within me? Hope in God, for I shall again praise Him, the help of my countenance, and my God" (Psalm 43:5).

If Satan can't destroy your concept of God, then he will seek to destroy your concept of who you are as a child of God. He can't do anything about your position in Christ, but if he can get you to believe it's not true, you will live as if it's not, even though it is. The two most important beliefs you possess are who God is and who you are as His child.

Unmet Spiritual Needs

*The world is passing away, and also its lusts; but the
one who does the will of God abides forever.*

1 JOHN 2:17

Over the last several decades, people in the West have begun to sense that there is more to life than science has revealed and their senses have experienced—and, of course, they're right. On the surface this new hunger may sound encouraging to those of us with a Christian worldview, but in fact the same people who are disillusioned with the materialistic world are also disillusioned with established religion. Instead of turning to Christ and His church, they are filling their spiritual void with old-fashioned occultism dressed in the modern garb of parapsychology, holistic health, Eastern mysticism, and numerous cults marching under the banner of the New Age Movement.

Attempting to meet spiritual needs apart from God is nothing new. Christ encountered a secularized form of Judaism during His earthly ministry which was bound to its traditions instead of to the God of Abraham, Isaac, and Jacob. The religious leaders of the day didn't recognize the Messiah as their spiritual deliverer. They perceived the oppressor to be Rome, not Satan, the god of this world. But Jesus came to undo the works of Satan (1 John 3:8), not Caesar.

Satan's ultimate lie is that you are capable of being the god of your own life, and his ultimate bondage is getting you to live as though his lie is true. Satan is out to usurp God's place in your life. And whenever you live independently of God, focusing on yourself instead of the cross, preferring material and temporal values to spiritual and eternal values, he has succeeded. The world's solution to this conflict of identity is to inflate the ego while denying God the opportunity to take His rightful place as Lord. Satan couldn't be more pleased—that was his plan from the beginning.

Demonstrating What We Believe

Even so faith, if it has no works, is dead, being by itself.
JAMES 2:17

Faith is an action word. We cannot passively respond to God. You may have heard the story of the circus performer who strung a wire over a river and proceeded to ride across it on a unicycle. When he returned, everyone applauded. Then he asked, "Who believes I can do that with a man on my shoulders?" Everyone responded in affirmation. He said, "All right, who will hop on?" The person who hops on is the person who really believes. Faith is not just giving credence to something or someone. Faith is demonstrated reliance upon something or someone.

Faith has the same operating dynamic as *agape* love. When we refer to love as a noun, we're talking about character: patience, kindness, etc. (1 Corinthians 13:4-7). When we say that God is love, we are describing His character. Paul says the goal of our instruction is love (1 Timothy 1:5); therefore, the goal of Christian education is character transformation.

When love is used as a verb, it is expressed by action: "For God so loved the world, that He gave…" (John 3:16). If we say we love someone and do nothing on their behalf, it's only sentimentality and not *agape* love. True love is expressed by meeting the needs of others.

Faith has a similar dynamic. When using faith as a noun, we're talking about what we believe. But if we're talking about faith as a verb, then it is expressed in the way we live. James says it like this: "Even so faith, if it has no works, is dead, being by itself. But someone may well say, 'You have faith, and I have works; show me your faith without the works, and I will show you my faith by my works.' You believe that God is one. You do well; the demons also believe, and shudder" (James 2:17-19).

The devil believes in the existence of Jesus and knows that God's Word is true. But he doesn't seek to glorify Jesus or to obey Him. He seeks his own glory, being a rebel at heart (Romans 1:25).

We demonstrate what we believe by how we live our lives. If we believe it, we will do it. If we don't, then what we believe is just wishful thinking.

Healing Confession

Confess your sins to one another and pray for
one another, that you may be healed.

JAMES 5:16 ESV

In this verse, James is referring to being healed from those illnesses that are directly related to sin, which usually fall in the category of what the secular medical profession calls psychosomatic illnesses. A lot more people are sick for psychosomatic reasons than we often realize. "Beloved, I pray that all may go well with you and that you may be in good health, as it goes well with your soul" (3 John 2 ESV). If it's not going well with our soul, it's likely we'll have health issues.

According to Paul, not judging ourselves rightly "is why many of you are weak and ill, and some have died" (1 Corinthians 11:30 ESV). Bitterness and unmanaged anger can be the basis for high blood pressure and heart attacks. It's a false hope to believe that the prayers of someone else will heal our illnesses if we're eating the wrong foods in excess and we never exercise or get adequate rest. When an encourager helps an inquirer resolve their personal and spiritual conflicts, then "the prayer of a righteous person has great power as it is working" (James 5:16 ESV). The Bible tells us that "a joyful heart is good medicine, but a crushed spirit dries up the bones" (Proverbs 17:22 ESV).

Other illnesses come from living in a fallen world, natural aging, and unfortunate accidents. For these we need to hold up one another in prayer.

Perceptions and Emotions

The LORD's lovingkindnesses indeed never cease, for His compassions never fail. They are new every morning; great is Thy faithfulness.
LAMENTATIONS 3:22-23

In a general sense, your emotions are a product of your thought life. If you are not thinking right, if your mind is not being renewed, if you are not perceiving God and His Word properly, it will be reflected in your emotional life.

One of the best scriptural illustrations of the relationship between perceptions and emotions is found in Lamentations 3. In verses 1-6, Jeremiah expresses despair as he wrongly perceives that God is against him and that He is the cause of his physical problems. In verses 7-11, 18, he vents his feelings of entrapment and fear. If your hope was in God, and these words were a correct portrayal of God, you would probably feel bummed out too.

What was Jeremiah's problem? His perception of God was way off. God wasn't the cause of his affliction. God isn't waiting to chew people up. But Jeremiah wasn't thinking right, perceiving right, or interpreting his circumstances right, so he wasn't feeling or responding right.

Suddenly, Jeremiah's countenance changes: "This I recall to my mind, therefore I have hope. The LORD's lovingkindnesses indeed never cease, for His compassions never fail. They are new every morning; great is Thy faithfulness" (verses 21-23). What a turnaround! Did God change? Did Jeremiah's circumstances change? No. His perception of God changed and his emotions followed suit.

You are not shaped so much by your environment as you are by your perception of it. Life's events don't determine who you are; God determines who you are, and your interpretation of life's events determines how well you handle life. Our thoughts determine our feelings and our responses. That's why you need to fill your mind with the knowledge of God and His Word. You need to see life from God's perspective and respond accordingly.

The Power to Choose

Choose for yourselves today whom you will serve...
As for me and my house, we will serve the LORD.
JOSHUA 24:15

Adam and Eve's sin also affected the area of their will. Do you realize that in the Garden of Eden they could only make one wrong choice? Everything they wanted to do was okay except eating from the tree of the knowledge of good and evil (Genesis 2:16-17). They had the possibility of making a myriad of good choices and only one bad choice—*only one!*

Eventually, however, they made that one bad choice. As a result, you and I are confronted every day with a myriad of good and bad choices. You can choose to pray or not pray, read your Bible or not read your Bible, go to church or not go to church. You can choose to walk according to the flesh or according to the Spirit. You and I face countless choices like that every day, and we eventually make some bad ones.

Other than the Holy Spirit in your life, the greatest power you possess is the power to choose. Someone has said that pure Christianity lies in the exercise of the will. The animal kingdom operates out of divine instinct. But we are created in the image of God, which means we have a self-operated, independent will. The essence of temptation is to function independently of God. The basis for temptation is legitimate needs.

Sinful behavior is often a wrong attempt at meeting your basic needs. The real issue here is are you going to get your needs met by the world, the flesh, and the devil, or are you going to allow God to meet all your needs "according to His riches in glory in Christ Jesus" (Philippians 4:19)? It's an issue of identity and maturity. The more you understand your identity in Christ, the more you will grow in maturity. And the more mature you become, the easier it will be for you to choose to live your life in dependence on your heavenly Father.

His Accepted, Adopted Child

Beloved, now we are children of God.

1 JOHN 3:2

Having a right relationship with God begins with settling once and for all the issue that God is your loving Father and you are His accepted, adopted child. That's the foundational truth of your spiritual heritage. You are a child of God, you are created in His image, you have been declared righteous by Him because you trust that what Christ accomplished in His death and resurrection is applicable to you. As long as you believe that and walk accordingly, your daily experience of practical Christianity will result in growth. But when you forget who you are and try to gain in your daily experience the acceptance God has already extended to you, you'll struggle. We don't serve God to gain His acceptance; we are accepted, so we serve God. We don't follow Him in order to be loved; we are loved, so we follow Him.

That's why you are called to live by faith (Romans 1:16-17). The essence of the victorious Christian life is believing what is already true about you. Do you have a choice? Of course! Satan will try to convince you that you are an unworthy, unacceptable, sin-sick person who will never amount to anything in God's eyes. Is that who you are? No, you are not! You are a saint whom God has declared righteous. Believing Satan's lie will lock you into a defeated, fruitless life. But believing God's truth about your identity will set you free.

Your perception of your identity makes such a big difference in your success at dealing with the challenges and conflicts of your life. It is imperative to your growth and maturity that you believe God's truth about who you are.

The Bible says, "See how great a love the Father has bestowed upon us, that we should be called children of God; and such we are" (1 John 3:1). Tragically, many believers are desperately trying to become something they already are, while others are living like something they aren't. It's true: "Beloved, now we are children of God" (1 John 3:2).

Authority and Power

[Jesus] called the twelve together, and gave them
power and authority over all the demons.

Luke 9:1

Jesus gave His disciples both *authority* and *power* over demons. What's the difference? Authority is the *right* to rule; it's a positional issue. A policeman has the right to stop traffic at an intersection because of the position of authority represented by his badge. Similarly, Jesus gave His disciples His badge to carry. They had the right to rule over the demons because of their position as followers of the One to whom all authority in heaven and on earth has been given (Matthew 28:18).

In contrast, power is the *ability* to rule. A policeman may have the authority to stop traffic, but he doesn't have the physical ability to do so. If he tries to stop traffic by his own power, he will probably get run over. However, if you move a 20-foot-square cement block into the middle of the intersection, it may not have any authority to make cars stop, but it certainly has the ability to do so!

No good manager would delegate *responsibility* to his subjects without also delegating *authority* to them and equipping them with the *ability* to get the job done. Jesus charged His disciples with the *responsibility* to proclaim the kingdom of God. Had He not also given them *authority and power* in the spirit world, the demons would have just scoffed at their feeble attempts and sent them running for cover (as they did the seven sons of Sceva in Acts 19).

The truth is that, while in yourself you don't have the ability to resist Satan and his demons, *in Christ you do*. The Israelites looked at Goliath fearfully and said, "We can't fight him." But young David looked at Goliath and said, "Who is this uncircumcised Philistine, that he should taunt the armies of the living God?" (1 Samuel 17:26). The army saw Goliath in relation to themselves and trembled; David saw Goliath in relation to God and triumphed. When you encounter the spiritual enemies of your soul, remember: "Be strong in the Lord [your authority], and in the strength of His might [your power]" (Ephesians 6:10).

Uninhibited Spontaneity

Shout joyfully to the LORD, all the earth. Serve the LORD
with gladness; come before Him with joyful singing.
PSALM 100:1-2

Have you ever planned a major fun event and then asked yourself, *Are we having fun yet?* Fun is uninhibited spontaneity. Chances are the last time you really had fun it was a spontaneous, spur-of-the-moment activity or event. Big events and expensive outings can be fun, but sometimes we plan and spend all the fun right out of them. I've often had a lot more fun in an impromptu pillow fight with my children.

The secret to enjoying uninhibited spontaneity as a Christian is in removing non-scriptural inhibitors. Chief among the inhibitors of Christian fun is our fleshly tendency to keep up appearances. We don't want to look out of place or be thought less of by others, so we stifle our spontaneity with a form of false decorum. That's people-pleasing, and Paul suggested that anybody who lives to please people isn't serving Christ (Galatians 1:10).

I really like the uninhibited joy I see in King David, who knew the joy of being in the presence of the Lord. He was so happy about returning the ark to Jerusalem that he leaped and danced before the Lord in celebration. He knew there was joy in the presence of God. But Michal, his party-pooping wife, thought his behavior was unbecoming to a king, and she told him so in no uncertain terms. David said, "Rain on you, lady. I'm dancing to please the Lord, not you or anybody else. And I'm going to keep dancing whether you like it or not" (my paraphrase of 2 Samuel 6:21). As it turned out, Michal was the person God judged in the incident, not David (2 Samuel 6:23). You'll find a lot more joy in pleasing the Lord than in trying to please people.

Frankly, I think it's fun being saved. Being free in Christ means that we are free to be ourselves. We're free from our past, free from trying to live up to other people's expectations, free from sin and the evil one. What a joyful, uninhibited, spontaneous life for those who are free in Christ!

Your Advocate

*Christ is the atoning sacrifice for our sins, and not only
for ours but also for the sins of the whole world.*
1 JOHN 2:2 NIV

Mandy appeared to have her life all together. She was a Christian who was very active in her church. She had led her alcoholic father to Christ. She was pretty, and she had a nice husband and two wonderful children. But she had attempted suicide at least three times.

"How can God love me?" Mandy sobbed. "I'm such a failure."

"Mandy, God loves you, not because you are lovable, but because it is His nature to love you."

"But I've tried to take my own life, Neil. How can God overlook that?"

"Just suppose, Mandy, that your son tried to take his own life. Would you love him any less? Would you turn your back on him?"

"Of course not. I'd feel sorry for him and try to love him more."

"Are you telling me that a perfect God isn't as good a parent to you as you, an imperfect person, are to your children?"

Mandy got the point. She began to realize that God, as a loving parent, can overlook weaknesses and forgive sin.

God wants us to do good, of course. The apostle John wrote: "I write this to you so that you will not sin." But John continued by reminding us that God has already made provision for our failure so His love continues constant despite what we do: "But if anybody does sin, we have one who speaks to the Father in our defense—Jesus Christ, the Righteous One. He is the atoning sacrifice for our sins, and not only for ours but also for the sins of the whole world" (1 John 2:1-2 NIV).

One reason we doubt God's love is that we have an adversary who uses every little offense to accuse us of being good-for-nothings. But your advocate, Jesus Christ, is more powerful than your adversary. He has canceled the debt of your sins past, present, and future. No matter what you do or how you fail, God has no reason not to love you and accept you completely.

Living Above Life's Circumstances

I have learned to be content in whatever circumstances I am.

PHILIPPIANS 4:11

Some of us tend to assume that it is God's will if the circumstances are favorable and it isn't God's will if the circumstances are unfavorable. Next to the Bible, I would guess that more Christians are "guided" by this means than any other. Yet of all the possible means of guidance, this is the least authoritative and trustworthy.

I had the privilege of pastoring a church that purchased new property and went through a building program. Through most of the process the circumstances didn't seem favorable. Twice I sat with the mayor, who was also a local real estate agent, and asked him if he thought our plans were feasible. He advised us not to make the land trade, and he didn't think the city would allow us to build. He knew the real estate and the political climate better than anyone in the city. But the land swap increased our assets by millions and the city planning commission voted 7-0 in favor of our building plans.

You may have to set sail by the tide, but you'd better be guided by the stars or you're going to end up on the wrong shore. Circumstances may have their effect on your plans, but you have a far greater accountability to God. Make sure you follow Him, not the tide of circumstance.

I heard a motivational speaker say, "I don't like to recruit Christians because when the going gets tough they quit, concluding that it must not be God's will." Generally speaking, I believe that Christians should live above life's circumstances and not be guided by them.

Also be careful about applying too much significance to unusual circumstances or coincidences. *It must be God's will. Why else would that book be lying there!* It could be God's will, but I would never take that kind of a sign on its own merit. I have helped many people in occultic bondage who have made bizarre associations or attached far too much significance to irrelevant events.

A Liberating Friend

*Surely you desire truth in the inner parts; you
teach me wisdom in the inmost place.*
PSALM 51:6 NIV

Absolute truth is the revelation of God's Word, and we must live that
truth in the inner self. When David lived a lie he suffered greatly.
When he finally found freedom by acknowledging the truth, he wrote,
"How blessed is the man…in whose spirit there is no deceit" (Psalm
32:2). Later, he wrote, "Surely you desire truth in the inner parts; you
teach me wisdom in the inmost place" (Psalm 51:6 NIV).

We are to lay aside falsehood and speak the truth in love (Ephesians
4:15, 25). A mentally healthy person is one who is in touch with reality
and relatively free of anxiety. Both qualities should epitomize the Christian who renounces deception and embraces the truth.

Deception is the most subtle of all satanic strongholds. Have you
ever noticed that all people with addictive behavior lie to themselves
and others almost continuously? The alcoholic lies about their drinking, the anorexic lies about their eating, and the sex offender lies about
their behavior. Lying is an evil defense prompted by the father of lies,
Satan (John 8:44).

The first step in any recovery program is to get out of denial and
face the truth. Truth is never an enemy; it is always a liberating friend.
People in bondage to the lie grow weary of the darkness. They hate to
sneak around, lie, and cover up. "God is light, and in Him there is no
darkness at all" (1 John 1:5). We must "walk in the light as He Himself
is in the light" (1 John 1:7). There is great freedom when truth dispels
the anguish of living a lie.

Choosing the truth may be difficult if you have been living a lie
for many years. You may need to seek professional help to weed out
the defense mechanisms you have depended on to survive. The Christian needs only one defense: Jesus. Knowing that you are forgiven and
accepted as God's child sets you free to face reality and choose the truth.

Spiritual War

I will remain in the world no longer, but they are still in the world, and I am coming to you. Holy Father, protect them by the power of your name.
JOHN 17:11 NIV

The Christian worldview perceives life through the grid of Scripture, not through culture or experience. And Scripture clearly teaches that supernatural, spiritual forces are at work in the natural world. For example, approximately one-fourth of all the healings recorded in the Gospel of Mark were actually deliverances from demon activity. The woman whom Jesus healed in Luke 13:11-12 had been the victim of a "sickness caused by a spirit" for 18 years.

Many people I have counseled came with physical problems which disappeared shortly after the demonic influence was dealt with. The most common symptoms I have seen are headaches, dizziness, allergies, nausea, and general pain throughout the body. The most conservative estimate by medical doctors is that 50 percent of their patients are suffering psychosomatic illnesses. Biblically, it is reasonable to expect if a person's personal and spiritual problems are resolved, the physical body will be benefited. Stress is a leading cause of heart disease and cancer. The peace of God alone will cure many diseases.

I'm not saying that everyone who is ill or in pain is being terrorized by a demon. But I am convinced that many Christians battle physical symptoms unsuccessfully through natural means when the essence of the problem and the solution is spiritual. "He who raised Christ Jesus from the dead, will also give life to your mortal bodies through His Spirit who indwells you" (Romans 8:11).

The fact that Jesus left us "in the world" (John 17:11) to wrestle against "spiritual forces of wickedness in the heavenly places" (Ephesians 6:12) is a present-day reality. Supernatural forces are at work on planet Earth. We live in the natural world, but we are involved in a spiritual war.

How God Works

You shall keep the commandments of the LORD your
God, to walk in His ways and to fear Him.
DEUTERONOMY 8:6

I believe in miracles, and I accept as fact every one recorded in the Bible. I believe that our entire Christian experience is a miracle. It simply cannot be explained by natural means. And God's power is seen in other miraculous ways today, but must He always prove Himself by stepping outside His created order? If God doesn't primarily guide us through His Word (which never changes) and take into account the fixed order of the universe, how can we ever have any stability? How can we make any plans if God doesn't reveal His ways and then stay consistent with them?

God is not capricious in His dealings with humans. He has clearly established His ways and He is faithful to them. I believe God has revealed His ways and we are to walk in them. The question is, how does God work through human responsibility and the natural order of the universe to bring about His will? Somehow He works through a less-than-perfect church, orchestrating human affairs in such a way as to guarantee the outcome of the ages. What really impresses me is His timing, not His miraculous interventions.

Notice how Jesus responded to those who insisted on a sign: "An evil and adulterous generation craves for a sign; and yet no sign shall be given to it but the sign of Jonah the prophet" (Matthew 12:39). Satan wanted a sign too. He said, "If You are the Son of God throw Yourself down" (Matthew 4:6). To this Jesus responded, "Do not put the Lord your God to the test" (verse 7 NIV). Jesus was saying that the sign we need is the Word of God, and we are to use the Word to guard against Satan's temptations to force the Lord to prove Himself.

I think it is better to prove ourselves to God rather than demand He prove Himself to us. We are the ones being tested, not God. "Be diligent to present yourself approved to God as a workman who does not need to be ashamed, handling accurately the word of truth" (2 Timothy 2:15).

The Order of Scripture

*Do not lie to one another, seeing that you have put off the old
self with its practices and have put on the new self, which is
being renewed in knowledge after the image of its creator.*
COLOSSIANS 3:9-10 ESV

Each of Paul's Epistles generally follow the pattern of the indicative (something we need to know) before the imperative (something we need to do). The first half establishes us in Christ, and the second half is mostly instruction about living.

Biblically correct instruction can be given about marriage and family and still produce very little fruit if we're not first established in Christ. Telling an unrepentant husband and wife how to behave as spouses is like instructing two people on crutches how to dance.

If we first establish ourselves free in Christ, then we can live as Scripture instructs supernaturally. "Put on then, as God's chosen ones, holy and beloved, compassionate hearts, kindness, humility, meekness, and patience, bearing with one another and...forgiving each other" (Colossians 3:12-13 ESV). Following those verses are instructions for family and work, because God primarily works in our lives through committed relationships for two reasons.

First, we can be a phony in public but not manage phoniness so well at home. Family members will see through us. Second, the pressure cooker of home is where we're supposed to learn how to love and forgive one another. Rather than run away, we must stay committed to one another and grow up.

God's Protection

But resist [the devil], firm in your faith, knowing that the same experiences
of suffering are being accomplished by your brethren who are in the world.
1 PETER 5:9

I cannot accept someone saying, "The devil made me do it." No, he didn't make you do it; you did it. Somewhere along the line you chose to give the devil a foothold. He merely took advantage of the opportunity you gave him. You have all the resources and protection you need to live a victorious life in Christ every day. If you're not living it, it's your choice. When you leave a door open for the devil by not resisting temptation, accusation, or deception, you are vulnerable. And if you continue to allow him access to your life, he can gain a measure of control over you. You won't lose your salvation, but you will lose your daily victory.

Many Christians today who cannot control their lives in some area wallow in self-blame instead of acting responsibly to solve the problem. They berate themselves and punish themselves for not having the willpower to break a bad habit, when instead they should be resisting Satan in an area where he has obviously robbed them of control. Anything bad which you seemingly cannot stop doing, or anything good which you cannot make yourself do, could be an area of demonic control.

God's protection from demonic attack is not something you can take for granted irrespective of how you behave. This protection is conditional on your willingness to respond to God's provision. We are told to put on Christ and make no provision for the flesh (Romans 13:14), to put on the armor of God and to stand firm (Ephesians 6:11), to submit to God and resist the devil (James 4:7). If we irresponsibly ignore God's resources by failing to obey these commands, how can we expect Him to protect us?

The Value of Counsel

Where there is no guidance, the people fall, but in
abundance of counselors there is victory.
PROVERBS 11:14

No one person has complete knowledge, and everyone has limited perspective on the truth. God has structured the church in such a way that we need each other. I have made some dumb decisions that would never have been made if I had consulted someone. However, some people will only consult those who agree with them. That's a sign of immaturity.

At the same time, the counsel of others does have to be weighed. There is a fascinating account in Acts 21 where the Holy Spirit seemed to be warning Paul not to go to Jerusalem. Disciples in Tyre "kept telling Paul through the Spirit not to set foot in Jerusalem" (verse 4). Then a prophet named Agabus gave a visual demonstration by binding himself and saying, "This is what the Holy Spirit says: 'In this way the Jews at Jerusalem will bind the man who owns this belt [Paul] and deliver him into the hands of the Gentiles'" (verse 11).

Everyone began begging him not to go. "Then Paul answered, '...I am ready not only to be bound, but even to die at Jerusalem for the name of the Lord Jesus.' And since he would not be persuaded, we fell silent, remarking, 'The will of the Lord be done!'" (verses 13-14).

Was the Holy Spirit guiding the disciples and Agabus? The information was mostly true, but the conclusion of the disciples wasn't. The Holy Spirit wasn't trying to prevent Paul from going; He was preparing Paul for the coming persecution. Paul was right in not wanting to take the easy way out.

Sometimes people can tell you the truth, but they draw selfish conclusions. Sometimes we need to ascertain our motives as well as the motives of those who counsel us. The value of counsel is to get an unbiased opinion from a spiritually sensitive person which you can add to the recipe of ingredients God is giving to guide you.

Self-Centered vs. God-Centered

You are not setting your mind on God's interests, but man's.
MATTHEW 16:23

The apostle Peter is a glaring example of the struggle between self- and Christ-centered living. Only moments after Peter confessed the fundamental truth that Jesus Christ is the Messiah, the Son of the living God (Matthew 16:13-16), he found himself in league with the powers of darkness. Having just blessed Peter for his noble confession, Jesus announced to him and the other disciples the suffering and death which awaited Him at Jerusalem. "And Peter took Him aside and began to rebuke Him, saying, 'God forbid it, Lord! This shall never happen to You'" (verse 22).

Jesus responded: "Get behind Me, Satan! You are a stumbling block to Me; for you are not setting your mind on God's interests, but man's" (verse 23).

Jesus' memorable rebuke seems mercilessly severe. But the fact that He identified Satan as the source of Peter's words describes precisely and appropriately the character of the advice Peter tried to give: *Save yourself at all costs. Sacrifice duty to self-interest, the cause of Christ to personal convenience.* Peter's advice was satanic in principle, for Satan's primary aim is to promote self-interest as the chief end of mankind. Satan is called the "prince of this world" because self-interest rules the secular world. He is called the "accuser of the brethren" because he does not believe that even a child of God has a higher motive than self-service. You can almost hear him hissing, "All men are selfish at heart and have their price. Some may hold out longer than others, but in the end every man will prefer his own things to the things of God."

That's Satan's creed, and unfortunately the lives of all too many Christians validate his claims. Satan has deceived them into thinking they are serving themselves when in fact they are serving the world, the flesh, and the devil. But the Christian worldview has a different center. Jesus confronts our humanistic, self-serving grids and offers the view from the cross. Only from this center can you escape the bondage of the one whose sole intent is "to steal, and kill, and destroy" (John 10:10).

One Basis for Temptation

*Let our people also learn to engage in good deeds to meet
pressing needs, that they may not be unfruitful.*
TITUS 3:14

We all have basic human needs to feel loved, accepted, and worth-while. When these needs go unmet, it's very important that we express them to our family members and fellow Christians in a positive way and allow others to minister to those needs. I believe that one basis for temptation is unmet legitimate needs. When you are too proud to say, "I don't feel loved," or when you push others away by saying, "You don't love me anymore," your need for love goes unmet. So Satan comes along with a tempting alternative: "Your wife doesn't love you like you deserve. But have you noticed the affectionate gleam in your secretary's eye?"

Other than Himself, God's primary resource for meeting your needs and keeping you pure is other believers. The problem is that many go to Sunday school, church, and Bible study wearing a sanctimonious mask. Wanting to appear strong and together, they rob themselves of the opportunity of having their needs met in the warmth and safety of the Christian community. In the process, they rob the community of the opportunity to minister to their needs. By denying the fellowship of believers the privilege of meeting your legitimate needs, you are acting independently of God. You are vulnerable to the temptation of thinking that you can have your needs met in the world, the flesh, and the devil.

Instead, follow the guidance of Hebrews 10:24-25: "Let us consider how to stimulate one another to love and good deeds, not forsaking our own assembling together, as is the habit of some, but encouraging one another; and all the more, as you see the day drawing near."

Living in Harmony

I am convinced that neither death, nor life, nor angels, nor
principalities, nor things present, nor things to come, nor powers,
nor height, nor depth, nor any other created thing, shall be able to
separate us from the love of God, which is in Christ Jesus our Lord.
ROMANS 8:38-39

When I was born physically I had a father. As Marvin Anderson's son, is there anything that I could possibly do which would change my blood relationship to him? What if I ran away from home and changed my name? Would I still be his son? Of course! We're related by blood and nothing can change that. But is there anything I could do which would affect the harmony of our relationship as father and son? Yes, indeed! The harmony of our relationship was interrupted countless times by my behavior.

In the spiritual realm, when I was born again I became a member of God's family. God is my Father and I enjoy an eternal relationship with Him through the precious blood of Christ (1 Peter 1:18-19). I am a child of God, in spiritual union with Him by His grace which I received through faith. My relationship with God was settled when I was born into His family. But is there anything I can do that will interfere with the *harmony* of my relationship with God? Of course! Living in harmony with God is based on the same issue as harmony with my earthly father: obedience. When I don't obey God the harmony of our relationship is disturbed. I love my heavenly Father and I want to be in harmony with Him, so I strive to obey Him. But even when we are in disharmony because of my disobedience, my relationship with Him is not at stake because we are related by the blood of Jesus Christ.

Paul was convinced that nothing could separate him from the love of God (Romans 8:35-39). Jesus said, "My sheep listen to my voice; I know them, and they follow me. I give them eternal life, and they shall never perish; no one can snatch them out of my hand" (John 10:27-28 NIV). Focus on your obedience to God so you may live in harmony with Him.

Persevering Tribulations

Consider it all joy, my brethren, when you encounter various trials,
knowing that the testing of your faith produces endurance.
JAMES 1:2-3

There certainly are a lot of distractions, diversions, disappointments, trials, temptations, and traumas which come along to disrupt the process of becoming the person God wants you to be. Every day you struggle against the world, the flesh, and the devil, each of which are opposed to your success at being God's person.

But Paul reminds us that the tribulations we face are actually a means of achieving our supreme goal of maturity: "We also exult in our tribulations, knowing that tribulation brings about perseverance; and perseverance, proven character; and proven character, hope; and hope does not disappoint, because the love of God has been poured out within our hearts through the Holy Spirit who was given to us" (Romans 5:3-5). James offers similar encouragement: "Consider it all joy, my brethren, when you encounter various trials, knowing that the testing of your faith produces endurance. And let endurance have its perfect result, that you may be perfect and complete, lacking in nothing" (James 1:2-4).

Maybe you thought your goal as a Christian was to escape tribulations. But God's goal for you is maturity in Christ, becoming the person He designed you to be. And tribulation just happens to be one of the primary stepping-stones on the pathway. That's why Paul says we exult—meaning to express heightened joy—in our tribulations. Why? Because persevering tribulations is the doorway to proven character, which is God's goal for us.

Our hope lies in proven character, not in favorable circumstances nor in the manipulation of others. Neither circumstances nor people can keep you from being who God wants you to be. Trials and tribulations are the most common means for bringing about His goal for your life.

Only God Is God

The serpent said… "You will be like God, knowing good and evil."
GENESIS 3:4-5

Adam was the first to be tempted by the notion that he could "be like God" (Genesis 3:5), which is the essence of the self-centered worldview that Satan promotes. Millions have been seduced by Satan into believing that they are God. The New Age Movement is promoting this lie on a grand and international scale.

However, the biblical account of creation clearly establishes that only God the Creator is truly God. Adam and his descendants are not gods; we are created beings who cannot exist apart from God. The diabolical idea that man is his own god is the primary link in the chain of spiritual bondage to the kingdom of darkness.

The problem with man's attempt at being his own god is that he was never designed to occupy that role. He lacks the necessary attributes to determine his own destiny. Even sinless, spiritually alive Adam in the Garden of Eden before the Fall wasn't equipped to be his own god. Contrary to what the New Agers tell us, the potential to be a god never was in you, isn't in you now, and never will be in you. Being God is God's capacity alone.

If you desire to live in freedom from the bondage of the world, the flesh, and the devil, this primary link in the chain must be renounced. The self-centered worldview which Satan and his emissaries are promoting must be replaced by the perspective that Jesus introduced to His disciples in the wake of Peter's self-preserving rebuke in Matthew 16: "If anyone wishes to come after Me, let him deny himself, and take up his cross, and follow Me. For whoever wishes to save his life shall lose it; but whoever loses his life for My sake shall find it" (verses 24-25). In the next several devotions we will examine the view from the cross.

Denying Self

If anyone wishes to come after Me, let him deny himself.
MATTHEW 16:24

A primary reason why we struggle to fulfill Christ's Great Commission is because we are guilty of a great *omission*: We fail to deny ourselves.

Denying yourself is not the same as self-denial. Students, athletes, and cult members practice self-denial, restricting themselves from substances and activities which keep them from reaching their goals. But the ultimate purpose of self-denial is self-glorification. The ultimate purpose of denying self is to glorify God.

Jesus was talking about denying yourself in the essential battle of life: the scramble for the throne, the struggle over who is going to be God. Jesus doesn't enter into that battle; He's already won it. He occupies the throne and graciously offers to share it with us. But we want to be king in our lives by ourselves. Until we deny ourselves that which was never meant to be ours—the role of being God in our lives—we will never be at peace with ourselves or God, and we will never be free.

You were not designed to function independently of God, nor was your soul designed to function as master. You will either serve God and His kingdom or Satan and his kingdom. Self-seeking, self-serving, self-justifying, self-glorifying, self-centered, and self-confident living is in actuality living and serving the world, the flesh, and the devil. On the other hand, denying yourself is not self-mortification. God is not trying to annihilate you; He is trying to restore you.

When you deny yourself, you invite God to take the throne of your life, to occupy what is rightfully His, so that you may function as a person who is spiritually alive in Christ. Denying yourself is essential to spiritual freedom.

Picking up the Cross Daily

If anyone wishes to come after Me, let him…take up his cross.
MATTHEW 16:24

The cross we are to pick up on a daily basis is not our own cross but Christ's cross. We are closely identified with His cross, however, because we have been crucified with Christ and no longer live; Christ lives in us (Galatians 2:20). His cross provided forgiveness from what we have done and deliverance from what we were. We are forgiven because He died in our place; we are delivered because we died with Him. We are both justified and sanctified as a result of the cross.

To pick up the cross daily means to acknowledge every day that we belong to God. We have been purchased by the blood of the Lord Jesus Christ (1 Peter 1:18-19). When we pick up the cross, we affirm that our identity is not based in our physical existence but in our relationship with God. We are identified as children of God (1 John 3:1-3) and our life is in Christ, who is our life (Colossians 3:3-4).

As a result of this acknowledgment, we stop trying to do our own thing in order to live daily to please our heavenly Father. We stop trying to become something we aren't, and we rest in the finished work of Christ, who made us something very special.

Jesus said, "Whoever wishes to save his [natural] life shall lose it; but whoever loses his life for My sake shall find it" (Matthew 16:25). Those who strive to establish their identity and seek to establish purpose and meaning in their natural life will someday lose it. We can't take it with us! We must take up our cross daily by acknowledging that life only finds meaning in Christ.

Following Him

If anyone wishes to come after Me, let him…follow Me.
MATTHEW 16:24

Seeking to overcome self by self-effort is a hopeless struggle. Self will never cast out self, because an independent self motivated by the flesh still wants to be God. We must follow Christ by being led by the Holy Spirit down the path of death to self-rule. As Paul wrote: "We who live are constantly being delivered over to death for Jesus' sake, that the life of Jesus also may be manifested in our mortal flesh" (2 Corinthians 4:11).

This may sound like a dismal path to walk, but I assure you that it is not. It is a tremendous experience to be known by the Shepherd and to follow Him as obedient, dependent sheep (John 10:27). The fact that we are led by the Spirit of God, even when it results in the death to self-rule, is our assurance of sonship (Romans 8:14). We were not designed to function independently of God. Only when we are dependent on Him and intent on following Christ are we complete and free to prove that the will of God is good, acceptable, and perfect (Romans 12:2).

Self-rule is motivated by self-interest and supported only by self-centered resources. When we come to the end of our resources, we discover God's resources. God will let us do our thing and patiently wait until self-interest and self-rule leave us spiritually and emotionally bankrupt. We can turn to God any time we weary of trying to run our own lives independently of Him. He doesn't force Himself on us, He just simply says, "If anyone wishes to come after Me, let him…follow Me." Are you willing to forsake self-rule and follow Him?

This View from the Cross

Whoever wishes to save his life shall lose it; but whoever loses
his life for My sake shall find it. For what will a man be
profited, if he gains the whole world, and forfeits his soul?
MATTHEW 16:25-26

Three guidelines from these verses summarize the view from the cross, which we must adopt to counteract the self-centered world-view promoted by the god of this world.

First, we must sacrifice the lower life to gain the higher life. If you want to save your natural life (i.e., find your identity and sense of self-worth in positions, titles, accomplishments, and possessions, and seek only worldly well-being) you will lose it. At best you can only possess these temporal values for a lifetime, only to lose everything for eternity.

Furthermore, in all your efforts to possess these earthly treasures, you will fail to gain all that can be yours in Christ. Shoot for this world and that's all you'll get, and eventually you will lose even that. But shoot for the next world and God will throw in the benefits of knowing Him in this present life as well. Paul put it this way: "Discipline yourself for the purpose of godliness; for bodily discipline is only of little profit, but godliness is profitable for all things, since it holds promise for the present life and also for the life to come" (1 Timothy 4:7-8).

Second, sacrifice the pleasure of things to gain the pleasure of life. What would you accept in trade for the fruit of the Spirit in your life? What material possession, position, or amount of money would you exchange for the love, joy, peace, and patience that you enjoy in Christ? *Nothing*, we all probably agree. Victory over self comes as we learn to love people and use things instead of using people and loving things.

Third, sacrifice the temporal to gain the eternal. Possibly the greatest sign of spiritual maturity is the ability to postpone rewards. It is far better to know that we are the children of God than to gain anything that the world calls valuable. Even if following Christ results in hardships in this life, He will make it right in eternity.

Righting Wrongs

By this is My Father glorified, that you bear much
fruit, and so prove to be My disciples.
JOHN 15:8

How can you know if you're being led by the Spirit or the flesh? Very simple: Look at your behavior. If you respond to a given situation by exercising love, joy, peace, patience, kindness, goodness, faithfulness, gentleness, and self-control, you are following the Spirit's lead (Galatians 5:22-23). If your reactions and responses reflect the deeds of the flesh listed in Galatians 5:19-21, you are following the flesh.

What do you do when you discover you are not walking by the Spirit? Acknowledge it for what it is. You have consciously or unconsciously chosen to live independently of God by walking according to the flesh. Walking according to the Spirit is a moment-by-moment, day-by-day experience. Acknowledge your sin to God, seek the forgiveness of anyone you may have offended, receive forgiveness, and be filled with the Spirit.

When you are faced with righting fleshly wrongs, here's what to do:

First, the scope of your confession should only be as broad as the scope of your offense. If you lashed out at a relative with angry words, you need only confess to God and that relative. If you entertain a secret, lustful thought or proud attitude without any overt, offensive behavior, you need only confess it to God. Confession literally means to agree with God. When you recognize an internal fleshly response, immediately acknowledge it in your mind. That's it; just agree with God and walk in the light.

Second, the process of restoring a relationship through confession and forgiveness is a step of spiritual growth. Your role as a spouse, parent, friend, coworker, or fellow-Christian is to model growth, not perfection. If you're trying to keep up a front of Christian perfection, forget it; it will never happen. But when you openly admit and ask forgiveness for your fleshly choices, you model the kind of spiritual growth which will touch saints and sinners alike.

Those Who Oppose Us

Our struggle is not against flesh and blood, but against the rulers,
against the powers, against the world forces of this darkness, against
the spiritual forces of wickedness in the heavenly places.
EPHESIANS 6:12

Virtually all evangelical Christians agree that Satan is a living being who is an evil force in the world. Historically, Christian confessions of faith have always included statements about belief in a personal devil—not that every person has his own personal devil, but that the devil is an actual personage rather than merely an impersonal force. But when you talk about demons being alive and active in the world today, a lot of Christians bristle, *Hold on there. I believe in the devil, but I don't buy that stuff about demons.*

My question to these people is: How do you think Satan carries on his worldwide ministry of evil and deception? He is a created being. He is not omnipresent, omniscient, or omnipotent. He can't be everywhere in the world tempting and deceiving millions of people at the same moment. He does so through an army of emissaries (demons, evil spirits, fallen angels, etc.) who propagate his plan of rebellion around the world. It is clear from the context of Ephesians 6:12 that the rulers, powers, and forces which oppose us are spiritual entities in the heavenlies (the spiritual world).

Disbelief in personal demonic activity (or an inordinate fear of demons) is further evidence of the static that Satan perpetrates in our minds to distort the truth. In the classic *Screwtape Letters*, C.S. Lewis wrote: "There are two equal and opposite errors into which our race can fall about the devils. One is to disbelieve their existence. The other is to believe and feel an unhealthy interest in them. They themselves are equally pleased by both errors and hail a materialist or a magician with the same delight."[2]

Success in God's Eyes

Be careful to do according to all the law which Moses My
servant commanded you... Then you will have success.
JOSHUA 1:7-8

A helpful perspective of success in the Christian life is seen in Joshua's experience of leading Israel into the Promised Land. God said to him: "Be strong and very courageous; be careful to do according to all the law which Moses My servant commanded you; do not turn from it to the right or to the left, so that you may have success wherever you go. This book of the law shall not depart from your mouth, but you shall meditate on it day and night, so that you may be careful to do according to all that is written in it; for then you will make your way prosperous, and then you will have success" (Joshua 1:7-8).

Was Joshua's success dependent on other people or circumstances? Absolutely not. Success hinged entirely on his obedience. If Joshua believed what God said and did what God told him to do, he would succeed. Sounds simple enough, but God immediately put Joshua to the test by giving him a rather unorthodox battle plan for conquering Jericho. Marching around the city for seven days, then blowing a horn, wasn't exactly an approved military tactic in Joshua's day!

But Joshua's success was conditional on obeying God regardless of how foolish His plan seemed. As Joshua 6 records, Joshua's success had nothing to do with the circumstances of the battle and everything to do with obedience. That should be your pattern too. Accept God's goal for your life and follow it obediently.

Don't take this truth lightly. You can be successful if you commit yourself to being what God has called you to be and follow Him obediently. You can be successful in business and remain in God's will even when your competition conducts business under the table and cheats on taxes. You can run for public office and win with a campaign that doesn't compromise God's will. You can be a failure in the eyes of the world and a success in the eyes of God—and vice versa.

Casting Our Anxieties on Christ

*Humble yourselves, therefore, under the mighty hand of God so
that at the proper time he may exalt you, casting all your anxieties
on him, because he cares for you. Be sober-minded; be watchful.
Your adversary the devil prowls around like a roaring lion.*
1 PETER 5:6-8 ESV

Casting our anxiety on Christ begins with prayer. "The Lord is at
hand; do not be anxious about anything, but in everything by prayer
and supplication with thanksgiving let your requests be made known to
God" (Philippians 4:5-6 ESV). In other words, don't be double-minded
about anything. Rather, become single-minded by turning to God in
prayer. Then the peace of God "will guard your hearts and your minds
in Christ Jesus" (verse 7 ESV).

After submitting to God, resist the devil. If believers are paying attention to a deceiving spirit, they are double-minded and therefore anxious.
Anxiety is a question of trust and single vision. Jesus is saying, *Trust Me.
I take care of the birds and the lilies of the field, and you have "more value
than they"* (Matthew 6:26 ESV). So don't worry about tomorrow's needs
for food and clothing, because "your heavenly Father knows that you
need them all. But seek first the kingdom of God and his righteousness,
and all these things will be added to you" (verses 32-33 ESV).

The next step is to state the problem. A problem well stated is half
solved. Then divide the facts from the assumptions. People tend to
assume the worst. The process of worrying often takes a greater toll on
them than the negative consequences they worried about.

Determine what you have the right and the ability to control. You
are not responsible for that which you don't have the right and the ability to control. List what you're responsible for and assume that responsibility. Don't cast your responsibility onto Christ. He will throw it back.
Any residual anxiety probably exists because you're assuming responsibilities God never intended you to have.

Our Relationship to Sin

Consider yourselves to be dead to sin, but alive to God in Christ Jesus.
ROMANS 6:11

E ven though you are dead to sin, sin's strong appeal may still cause you to struggle with feeling that you are more alive to sin than you are to Christ. But Romans 6:1-11 teaches us that what is true of the Lord Jesus Christ is true of us in terms of our relationship to sin and death. God the Father allowed His Son to "be sin" in order that all the sins of the world—past, present, and future—would fall on Him (2 Corinthians 5:21). When He died on the cross, our sins were on Him. But when He rose from the grave, there was no sin on Him. When He ascended to the Father, there was no sin on Him. And today, as He sits at the Father's right hand, there is no sin on Him. Since we are seated in the heavenlies in Christ, we too have died to sin.

Christ already died to sin, and because you are in Him, you have died to sin too. Sin is still strong and appealing, but your relationship with sin has ended. I've met many Christians who are still trying to die to sin, and their lives are miserable and fruitless as a result because they are struggling to do something that has already been done. "For the law of the Spirit of life in Christ Jesus has set you free from the law of sin and of death" (Romans 8:2).

Romans 6:11 summarizes what we are to believe about our relationship to sin because of our position in Christ. It doesn't matter whether you feel dead to sin or not; you are to *consider* it so because it *is* so. People wrongly wonder, *What experience must I have in order for this to be true?* The only necessary experience is that of Christ on the cross, which has already happened. When we choose to believe what is true about ourselves and sin, and walk on the basis of what we believe, our right relationship with sin will work out in our experience. But as long as we put our experience before our belief, we will never fully know the freedom that Christ purchased for us on the cross.

Weep with Those Who Weep

Rejoice with those who rejoice, and weep with those who weep.
ROMANS 12:15

Early in my pastoral ministry I received one of those middle-of-the-night telephone calls that every pastor dreads:

"Pastor, our son has been in an accident. They don't expect him to live. Could you please come to the hospital?"

I arrived at the hospital about one in the morning. I sat with the parents in the waiting room hoping and praying for the best but fearing the worst. About 4:00 a.m. the doctor came out to give us the worst: "We lost him."

We were devastated. I was so tired and emotionally depleted that instead of offering them words of comfort, I just sat there and cried with them. I couldn't think of anything to say. I went home feeling that I had failed the family in their darkest hour.

Soon after the accident the young man's parents moved away. But about five years later they stopped by the church for a visit and took me out to lunch. "Neil, we'll never forget what you did for us when our son died," they said. "We knew you loved us because you cried with us."

One of our challenges in the ministry is in learning how to respond to others when they honestly acknowledge their feelings. I find a very helpful principle in the conversations between Job and his friends. Job said: "The words of one in despair belong to the wind" (Job 6:26). What people say in an emotional crisis is irrelevant, other than to convey how deeply hurt they are. We have a tendency to fixate on words and ignore the hurt. When grief-stricken Mary and Martha greeted Jesus with the news of Lazarus' death, He wept (John 11:35). Paul's words crystallize it for us: "Rejoice with those who rejoice, and weep with those who weep" (Romans 12:15). We are not supposed to instruct those who weep; we are supposed to weep with those who weep.

Christ, Our Ruler

You were dead in your trespasses and sins, in which you
formerly walked according to the course of this world,
according to the prince of the power of the air.
EPHESIANS 2:1-2

We live in a world which is under the authority of an evil ruler. Originally God created Adam and his family to rule over creation. But Adam forfeited his position of authority through sin, and Satan became the rebel holder of authority to whom Jesus referred as "the ruler of this world" (John 12:31; 14:30; 16:11). During Jesus' temptation, the devil offered Him "all the kingdoms of the world, and their glory" (Matthew 4:8) in exchange for His worship. Satan's claim that the earth "has been handed over to me, and I give it to whomever I wish" (Luke 4:6) was no lie. He took authority when Adam abdicated the throne of rulership over God's creation at the Fall. Satan ruled from Adam until the cross. The death, resurrection, and ascension of Christ secured forever the final authority for Jesus Himself (Matthew 28:18). That authority was extended to all believers in the Great Commission so that we may continue His work of destroying the works of the devil (1 John 3:8).

All of us were born spiritually dead and subject to the ruler that Paul called "the prince of the power of the air" (Ephesians 2:2). But when we received Christ, God "delivered us from the domain of darkness, and transferred us to the kingdom of His beloved Son" (Colossians 1:13). Our citizenship was changed from earth to heaven (Philippians 3:20). Satan is the ruler of this world, but he is no longer *our* ruler, for Christ is our ruler.

But as long as we live on the earth, we are still on Satan's turf. He will try to rule our lives by deceiving us into believing that we still belong to him. As aliens in a foreign, hostile kingdom, we need protection from this evil, deceptive, hurtful tyrant. Christ has not only provided protection from and authority over Satan, but He has equipped us with the Spirit of truth, the indwelling Holy Spirit, to guide us into all truth and help us discern the evil one's schemes (John 16:13).

Mental Strongholds

Though we walk in the flesh, we are not waging war according
to the flesh. For the weapons of our warfare are not of the
flesh but have divine power to destroy strongholds.

2 Corinthians 10:3-4 esv

In this passage, Paul isn't talking about defensive armor. He's talking about the offensive weapons of God that tear down mental strongholds—flesh patterns that were erected in our minds before we came to Christ. They are mental habit patterns of thought burned into our minds over time. Essentially, they are assimilated from the environment in which we were raised in two primary ways.

The first is by the experiences we had growing up, such as the family we were raised in, the school we attended, the friends we had, and the church we went to or didn't go to. The second is traumatic experiences such as the divorce of parents, incest, or rape. People are not in bondage to past traumas but they may be in bondage to the lies they believe as a result of the trauma—lies such as *I'm not good. God doesn't love me. It's all my fault.*

The devil will attempt to infiltrate our minds with these lies. Such lies are often deeply embedded in our subconscious. And some of our flesh patterns are defense mechanisms, such as lying, denial, blaming, and rationalization. Paul explains, that in the war "we destroy arguments and every lofty opinion raised against the knowledge of God, and take every thought captive to obey Christ" (2 Corinthians 10:5 esv). Satan's lies and worldly philosophies raised up against the knowledge of God are subjugated to Christ when we choose to believe the truth.

God doesn't change our past; He sets us free from it. Jesus came to set captives free and heal the wounds of the brokenhearted. We are transformed by the renewing of our minds.

Believing Truth Is a Choice

Without faith it is impossible to please Him, for he who comes to God must believe that He is, and that He is a rewarder of those who seek Him.

HEBREWS 11:6

Faith is the biblical response to the truth, and believing truth is a choice. Faith is something you *decide* to do, not something you *feel like doing*. Believing the truth doesn't make it true; it's true, so we believe it. The New Age Movement and the "name it and claim it" adherents are distorting the truth by saying that we create reality through what we believe. We can't *create* reality; we can only *respond to* reality.

Faith must have an object. It's not the idea that you merely "believe" that counts; it's what or who you *believe in* that counts. Everybody believes in something, and everybody walks by faith according to what he or she believes. But if what you believe isn't true, then how you live won't be right. Thus, "Faith comes from hearing, and hearing by the Word of Christ" (Romans 10:17).

Your faith is only as great as your knowledge of the object of your faith. If you have little knowledge of God and His Word, you will have little faith. That's why faith can't be pumped up. Any attempt to live by faith beyond what you absolutely know to be true is presumption. If you only believe what you feel, you will be led through life by one emotional impulse after another. The path of truth begins with the truth of God's Word. Believe the truth and walk by faith according to what you believe, and then your feelings will line up with what you think and how you behave.

We can't decide for ourselves what we would like to believe and then believe it, expecting God to respond to our faith. God is under no obligation to people. There is no way we can cleverly word a prayer in such a way that God must answer it. He is under obligation only to Himself. He will always stay true to Himself and keep His Word and His covenants with mankind. It is not our place to determine what is true or try to persuade God to capitulate to our will. He is the truth. We are to ask according to His will and desire His will above all else.

The Peace of God

Peace I leave with you; My peace I give to you;
not as the world gives, do I give to you.
JOHN 14:27

Peace on earth—that's what everybody wants. But nobody can guarantee external peace because nobody can control other people or circumstances. Nations sign and break peace treaties with frightening regularity. Couples lament that there would be peace in their home "if only he/she would shape up." No one can guarantee peace at home or on the job site. However, we should always strive to be peacemakers. Jesus said, "Blessed are the peacemakers, for they shall be called sons of God" (Matthew 5:9). Paul instructed, "If possible, so far as it depends on you, be at peace with all men" (Romans 12:18).

But let's face it: Peace with others isn't always possible, because peace doesn't just depend on us. Peace on earth is what we want; peace *with* God is what we have; the peace *of* God is what we need.

Peace *with* God is something you already have (Romans 5:1). It's not something you strive for; it's something you received when you were born again. The Prince of Peace reconciled you to God by shedding His own blood.

The peace *of* God is something you need to appropriate daily in your inner world in the midst of the storms which rage in the external world (John 14:27). There are a lot of things that can disrupt your external world because you can't control all your circumstances and relationships. But you *can* control the inner world of your thoughts by allowing the peace of Christ to rule in your heart on a daily basis (Colossians 3:15). There may be chaos all around you, but God is bigger than any storm. I keep a little plaque on my desk that reminds me: "Nothing will happen to me today that God and I cannot resolve."

The peace of Christ will rule in your heart when you "let the word of Christ richly dwell within you" (Colossians 3:16). And when you turn to Him in prayer, "the peace of God, which surpasses all comprehension, shall guard your hearts and your minds in Christ Jesus" (Philippians 4:7).

Praying by the Spirit

*The Spirit helps us in our weakness. For we do not know what
to pray for as we ought, but the Spirit himself intercedes for
us with groanings too deep for words. And he who searches
hearts knows what is the mind of the Spirit, because the Spirit
intercedes for the saints according to the will of God.*

ROMANS 8:26-27 ESV

Joel prophesied the coming of the Holy Spirit at Pentecost (Joel
2:28-32; Acts 2:17-21), which happened when Jesus was exalted at
the right hand of the Father (Acts 2:33). Pentecost was the beginning
of the church age, when every believer is born again by a simple act of
faith; baptized by the Holy Spirit into the body of Christ (1 Corinthians 12:13); indwelt perpetually by the Holy Spirit (Romans 8:38-39);
and sealed by the Holy Spirit (Ephesians 1:13-14). When we are filled
with the Holy Spirit, we sing a melody in our hearts to the Lord (5:19).

We really don't know how or what to pray for, but the Holy Spirit
does, and He helps us. The word *helps* in Greek is two prepositions before the word *take*. The Holy Spirit comes alongside, bears us up, and
takes us across to the other side. Any prayer that God the Holy Spirit
prompts us to pray is a prayer that God the Father is always going to
answer. He not only helps us pray; He intercedes for us according to
the will of God—and He is not the only member of the Trinity inter-
ceding for us. Jesus "is able to save to the uttermost those who draw
near to God through him, since he always lives to make intercession
for them" (Hebrews 7:25 ESV).

Knowing that we have two members of the Trinity praying for us
is especially pertinent when confronting "the spiritual forces of evil in
the heavenly places" (Ephesians 6:12 ESV). Paul defines our protective
armor, and then he concludes by saying "praying at all times in the
Spirit, with all prayer and supplication" (verse 18 ESV).

God's Ministry of Darkness

For we who live are constantly being delivered over to death for Jesus'
sake, that the life of Jesus also may be manifested in our mortal flesh.

2 CORINTHIANS 4:11

What is the point of troubled times in our lives? What is God trying to do? What is He trying to teach us? Peter wrote, "Beloved, do not be surprised at the fiery ordeal among you, which comes upon you for your testing, as though some strange thing were happening to you; but to the degree that you share the sufferings of Christ, keep on rejoicing; so that also at the revelation of His glory, you may rejoice with exultation" (1 Peter 4:12-13).

In God's ministry of testing, we learn a lot about ourselves. Whatever is left of simplistic advice such as "Read your Bible" or "Just work harder" or "Pray more" gets stripped away. Most people going through testing times would love to resolve the crisis, but they seemingly can't and don't know why.

In God's ministry of darkness we learn compassion. We learn to wait patiently with people. We learn to respond to the emotional needs of people who have lost hope. We weep with those who weep. We don't try to teach or instruct or advise. If God took away every external blessing and reduced our assets to nothing more than meaningful relationships, would that be enough to sustain us? Yes, I believe it would.

Perhaps God brings us to the end of our resources so we can discover the vastness of His. We don't hear many sermons about brokenness in our churches these days, yet in all four Gospels Jesus taught us to deny ourselves, pick up our cross daily, and follow Him. I don't know any painless way to die to ourselves, but I do know that it's necessary and that it's the best possible thing that could ever happen to us.

"No pain, no gain," says the body builder. Isn't that true in the spiritual realm as well (Hebrews 12:11)? Proven character comes from persevering through the tribulations of life (Romans 5:3-5). Every great period of personal growth in my life and ministry has been preceded by a major time of testing.

The Hidden Hurts

Search me, O God, and know my heart; try me and
know my anxious thoughts; and see if there be any hurtful
way in me, and lead me in the everlasting way.
PSALM 139:23-24

Many people have major traumas. Some have been abused to such an extent they have no conscious memory of their experiences. Others avoid anything that will stimulate those memories. All of these people have had their emotions traumatized—and many are stuck there. Unable to process those experiences, they have sought to survive and cope with life through defense mechanisms. Some live in denial, others rationalize or try to suppress the pain with food, drugs, or sex.

This is not God's way, however. God does everything in the light. You can always count on God to bring your past conflicts to the surface at the right time so everything can be brought into the light and dealt with. When a person's conflict is deeply traumatic, God allows that person to mature to the point where they are able to face the reality of the past. I have prayed with many that God would reveal what is keeping them in bondage—and God has answered those prayers. Why don't we pray this way more often in counseling? I'm disappointed at how often the "Wonderful Counselor" is left out of Christian ministry.

I am personally against drug-induced programs or hypnosis that attempt to restore a repressed memory by bypassing the mind of the person involved. Everything I read in Scripture about the mind challenges believers to be mentally active, not passive. Getting ahead of God in the healing process through drugs or hypnosis can throw some into a quagmire of despair they can't escape.

I believe the first step in God's answer for repressed trauma is found in Psalm 139:23-24. God knows about the hidden hurts within you which you may not be able to see. When you ask God to search your heart, He will expose those dark areas of your past and bring them to light at the right time.

Living with Sin's Consequences

Never take your own revenge, beloved, but leave room for the wrath of God, for it is written, "Vengeance is Mine, I will repay," says the Lord.

ROMANS 12:19

Forgiveness does not mean that you must tolerate sin. Isabel, a young wife and mother attending one of my conferences, told me of her decision to forgive her mother for continually manipulating her for attention. But Isabel tearfully continued, "She is no different. Am I supposed to let her keep ruining my life?"

No, forgiving someone doesn't mean that you must be a doormat to their continual sin. I encouraged Isabel to confront her mother lovingly but firmly, and tell her that she would no longer tolerate destructive manipulation. It's okay to forgive another's past sins and, at the same time, take a stand against future sins. Forgiving is not a codependent activity.

Forgiveness does not demand revenge or repayment for offenses suffered. *You mean I'm just supposed to let them off the hook?* you may argue. Yes, you let them off *your* hook realizing that they are not off God's hook. You may feel like exacting justice, but you are not an impartial judge. God is the just Judge who will make everything right (Romans 12:19). Your job is to extend the mercy of forgiveness and leave judgment up to God.

Forgiveness is agreeing to live with the consequences of another person's sin. Suppose that someone in your church says, "I have gossiped about you. Will you forgive me?" You can't retract gossip any easier than you can put toothpaste back into the tube. You're going to live with the gossip this person spread about you no matter how you respond to the gossiper.

We are all living with the consequences of another person's sin: Adam's. The only real choice we have in the matter is to live in the bondage of bitterness or in the freedom of forgiveness.

Relationships First

Owe nothing to anyone except to love one another; for
he who loves his neighbor has fulfilled the law.

ROMANS 13:8

Many people demonstrate that their need to win when trying to resolve conflicts with others is greater than their regard for relationships. Why is winning so important to us? Why must we always be right? The person who is driven to win, to be right, or to be first is insecure. Insecure people are driven to perform.

Security comes from relationships, not achievements. A secure person is a person who is comfortable with himself and others. It is easy to communicate with a secure person, but you often end up clashing with a driven person. Would you rather be a lover or an achiever? Which would you prefer your spouse, children, coworkers, and friends to be?

Relationships are more important than achievements to God. Jesus declared that the two greatest commandments are to love God and love people (Matthew 22:36-40). The purpose of the Word of God is to govern our relationships with God and others. If our achievements in life don't enhance our relationships with God, our spouse and children, and others, then we are not fulfilling God's commandments.

Is there ever a time when we need to assert ourselves in conflicts? Yes, we need to stand our ground on moral issues. But we never have the right to violate the fruit of the Spirit in doing so. If what you do can't be done in love and self-control, then maybe it's better left undone. And remember: Your authority does not increase with the volume of your voice. When you resort to shouting in conflict you are reacting in the flesh. You have lost control of the only person you can control: yourself.

Anyone who accomplishes something at the expense of people or elevates tasks over relationships will sow the seeds of their own destruction and the destruction of those around them. Governments, institutions, and organizations exist for the cause and needs of people. The Sabbath was made for man, not man for the Sabbath. How easy it is to turn our priorities upside down.

Temptation

Let no one say when he is tempted, "I am being tempted by God," for God cannot be tempted with evil, and he himself tempts no one. But each person is tempted when he is lured and enticed by his own desire.

JAMES 1:13-14 ESV

G od will test our faith, but He can't tempt us for that would be evil. Some question their salvation when they're bombarded by Satan's temptations, but it's not a sin to be tempted. Jesus was "tempted in all things as we are, yet without sin" (Hebrews 4:15 NASB1995). As long as we're physically alive in this present world, we will be tempted just like Jesus was. But He didn't sin, and we don't have to sin either.

Temptation is an enticement to live independently of God. Before we came to Christ, we were all conformed to this world. Our souls were not in union with God, and we had no knowledge of God and His ways. We learned to live independently of Him. This learned independence is the essential characteristic of what the Bible calls the flesh, or old nature. But Jesus modeled a life dependent on the heavenly Father: "I can do nothing on my own" (John 5:30 ESV); "I live because of the Father" (6:57 ESV); "I came not of my own accord, but he sent me" (8:42 ESV); "Now they know that everything that you have given me is from you" (17:7 ESV).

What tempts you might not tempt another, and vice versa. Temptations from without lack power unless a corresponding desire is within. Jesus said, "The ruler of the world is coming, and he has nothing in Me" (14:30 NASB1995). Identifying the fleshly desires within us is the key to overcoming the temptation to sin.

Channels of Temptation

*Do not love the world or the things in the world. If anyone loves
the world, the love of the Father is not in him. For all that is in
the world—the desires of the flesh and the desires of the eyes and
pride of life—is not from the Father but is from the world.*
1 JOHN 2:15-16 ESV

The desires of the flesh" are physical appetites that seek gratification
in this world. "The desires of the eyes" are our self-serving interests.
The "pride of life" relates to self-promotion and exaltation. Satan confronted Eve through those three channels of temptation. "The woman
saw that the tree was good for food, and that it was a delight to the eyes,
and that the tree was to be desired to make one wise" (Genesis 3:6 ESV).

Actually, there were no fleshly desires in Eve at the time because she
had not yet sinned, so Satan had to get at her through deception. He
questioned the will of God: "Did God actually say, 'You shall not eat
of any tree in the garden?'" (verse 1 ESV). Eve repeated God's command
when she responded, but she added "neither shall you touch it, lest you
die" (verse 3 ESV). Then Satan questioned the word of God: "You will
not surely die" (verse 4 ESV). Finally, he questioned the worship of God:
"You will be like God" (verse 5 ESV).

Those three channels are intended to destroy our dependence on
God, our confidence in God, and our obedience to God. Satan also confronted Jesus through those three channels of temptation.

Desires of the Flesh

Then Jesus was led by the Spirit into the wilderness to be tempted
by the devil. And after fasting forty days and forty nights, he was
hungry. And the tempter came and said to him, "If you are the
Son of God, command these stones to become loaves of bread."
MATTHEW 4:1-3 ESV

Satan wasn't pursuing Jesus to tempt Him, because there was nothing in Jesus to tempt (for God cannot be tempted—James 1:13). It
was the Holy Spirit who led Jesus into the wilderness to be tempted by
the devil. Jesus was alone, isolated, and physically depleted, which aptly
describes when we are most vulnerable. Satan wanted Jesus to use His
divine attributes independent of His heavenly Father to save Himself.

Later, that is what Peter wanted Jesus to do as well: "Jesus began to
show his disciples that he must go to Jerusalem and suffer many things
from the elders and chief priests and scribes, and be killed, and on the
third day be raised. And Peter took him aside and began to rebuke him,
saying, 'Far be it from you, Lord! This shall never happen to you'" (Matthew 16:21-22 ESV). This brought a swift reproof from Jesus: "Get behind
me, Satan! You are a hindrance to me. For you are not setting your mind
on the things of God, but on the things of man" (verse 23 ESV).

In the wilderness, when Satan wanted Jesus to turn stones into bread,
Jesus replied, "Man shall not live by bread alone, but by every word that
comes from the mouth of God" (4:4 ESV). Jesus quoted Scripture, but
what is often overlooked is the fact that He said it. The sword of the
Spirit is the spoken word.

Satan has no obligation to obey our thoughts. When tempted late at
night and alone in front of the television or computer, submit to God
and verbally resist the devil, and he will flee. There is no embarrassment
when you are alone.

Lust of the Eyes

Then the devil took him to the holy city and set him on the pinnacle of the temple and said to him, "If you are the Son of God, throw yourself down, for it is written, 'He will command his angels concerning you.'"
MATTHEW 4:5-6 ESV

Satan deceived Eve by raising doubt about God's word: "Did God actually say…?" (Genesis 3:1 ESV). He does the same with Jesus by doubting His legitimacy—"If you are the Son of God"—and additionally he tempts Jesus by misusing God's Word. In essence, Satan was saying, *In vain God has called You "Son" and has beguiled You by His gift. If this is not so, give us some proof that You are from that power.* But Jesus had no need to prove Himself, and He correctly quoted Scripture: "Again it is written, 'You shall not put the Lord your God to the test'" (verse 7 ESV).

God, if you are really there, would you do this one thing for me? We have already given in to the temptation if we begin our prayer with, *God, if…* Nor can we cleverly word our prayer so that God must capitulate to our will. He is under no obligation to prove Himself to us. The righteous shall live by faith in the Word of God and not demand that God prove Himself in response to our wishes, no matter how noble they may be. We are the ones being tested, not God.

"Then Gideon said to God, 'If you will save Israel by my hand, as you have said, behold, I am laying a fleece of wool on the threshing floor. If there is dew on the fleece alone, and it is dry on all the ground, then I shall know that you will save Israel by my hand, as you have said'" (Judges 6:36-37 ESV). The fleece wasn't a means of demonstrating faith; it was just the opposite. And it certainly wasn't a means to determine God's will. He had already told Gideon what to do. Gideon was questioning God's will, just as we do when we ask for a fleece when He has already shown us His will.

The Pride of Life

Again, the devil took him to a very high mountain and showed
him all the kingdoms of the world and their glory. And he said to
him, "All these I will give you, if you will fall down and worship
me." Then Jesus said to him, "Be gone, Satan! For it is written, 'You
shall worship the Lord your God and him only shall you serve.'"
MATTHEW 4:8-10 ESV

The third channel of temptation is to direct our own destiny, to rule our own world, to be our own god. Satan said to Eve, "God knows that in the day you eat from it your eyes will be opened, and you will be like God, knowing good and evil" (Genesis 3:5 NASB1995). In other words, Satan was saying, *God doesn't want You to eat from the tree because He's holding out on You.* Jesus didn't challenge Satan's right to offer Him the kingdoms of the world. Since he was the god of this world, they were his to offer.

But Jesus was not about to settle for anything less than the defeat of Satan. Jesus stepped out of eternity into time so we can step out of time into eternity. He not only came to give us life; He *is* our life (Colossians 3:4 ESV). He left us an example to follow in His steps, of which the hardest is considering another person more important than ourselves. Self-interest rules this world, and the crucifixion is the sternest possible rebuke to human selfishness.

By appealing to the pride of life, Satan intends to steer us away from the worship of God and destroy our obedience to Him. When we manipulate others to get ahead of them; when we lie on our resume; when we compromise our convictions to accomplish a goal; when we smear another to make ourselves look better—beware. That is the pride of life.

"Do nothing from rivalry or conceit, but in humility count others more significant than yourselves. Let each of you look not only to his own interests, but also to the interests of others. Have this mind among yourselves, which is yours in Christ Jesus" (Philippians 2:3-5 ESV).

Way of Escape

No temptation has overtaken you that is not common to man.
God is faithful, and he will not let you be tempted beyond
your ability, but with the temptation he will also provide
the way of escape, that you may be able to endure it.
1 CORINTHIANS 10:13 ESV

Like people who know how to taunt their siblings, Satan knows our flesh patterns. We can't put flesh patterns to death because "those who belong to Christ Jesus *have* crucified the flesh with its passions and desires. If we live by the Spirit, let us also keep in step with the Spirit" (Galatians 5:24-25 ESV).

In the past, we have made conscious choices and behaved accordingly. It takes about six weeks of routine behavior to establish a habit, which becomes a neural pathway in the brain. These mental habit patterns of thought have to be crucified and replaced by the truth. The brain is like the hardware in a computer system, whereas the mind is like the software. We can reprogram our minds, but we must be aware of "viruses," which are never accidental.

Temptation will try to get us to go down those old neural pathways in the brain. But instead of finding our own way of escape, we can submit to God the moment we sense the temptation, asking Him to fill us with His Holy Spirit. The way of escape is available the moment we sense the temptation, which begins with a thought. Thinking on a tempting thought will give rise to the old fleshly passions and desires. "Desire when it has conceived gives birth to sin" (James 1:15 ESV). We can't stop the birds from flying overhead, but we can stop them from building a nest in our hair. We must remember who we are and choose to think on that which is true. Being unable to do so signifies a lack of genuine repentance and faith in God.

Becoming the Person God Wants

But we all...are being transformed into the same image
from glory to glory, just as from the Lord, the Spirit.
2 Corinthians 3:18

When you begin to align your goals with God's goals and your desires with God's desires, you will rid your life of a lot of anger, anxiety, and depression. The homemaker who wants a happy, harmonious family is expressing a godly desire, but she cannot guarantee that it will happen. So she'd better not base her identity and sense of worth on it or she will be a basket case of anger or resentment toward her sometimes less-than-harmonious family.

Instead she could decide, "I'm going to be the wife and mother God wants me to be." That's a great goal! Is it impossible or uncertain? No, because it's also God's goal for her, and nothing is impossible with God. Who can block her goal? She's the only one who can. As long as she cooperates with God's goal for her, her success is assured.

"But what if my husband has a mid-life crisis or my kids rebel?" she may object. Problems like that aren't blocking her goal of being the wife and mother God wants her to be, but they will put her goal to a serious test. If her husband ever needs a godly wife, and if her children ever need a godly mother, it's in times of trouble. Family difficulties are merely new opportunities for her to fulfill her goal of being the woman God wants her to be.

The pastor whose worth is based on his goal to win his community for Christ, have the best youth ministry in town, or increase giving to missions by 50 percent is headed for a fall. These are worthwhile desires, but they are poor goals by which to determine his worth because they can be blocked by people or circumstances. Rather he could say, "I'm going to be the pastor God wants me to be." That's a great goal because nothing can block him from achieving it.

God's basic goal for your life is character development: becoming the person God wants you to be. Because it's a godly goal, no one can block it except you.

Five Hindrances

One who looks intently at the perfect law...not having become a forgetful hearer but an effectual doer, this man shall be blessed in what he does.
JAMES 1:25

While God has given us an infallible guide to life—His Word—the truth He wants us to follow for our freedom can be obscured by our bias and selfish indulgence. In the twenty-first-century Western church I see at least five major hindrances which affect our understanding and application of the Word of God.

First, *there is a tendency to make doctrine an end in itself.* Christian maturity is not understanding the principles of the Bible; Christian maturity is character. If what we come to accept as truth doesn't affect our love for God and man, something is radically wrong (1 Timothy 1:5). "Knowledge makes arrogant, but love edifies" (1 Corinthians 8:1).

Second, *we can learn a lot about God from Scripture and not know Him at all.* Before his conversion, Paul knew the law, but he didn't recognize God in Christ when he saw Him. We're not asked to fall in love with doctrine. We're asked to fall in love with the Lord Jesus Christ.

Third, *we often encourage memorizing Scripture instead of thinking scripturally.* Our model should be, "The Word became flesh, and dwelt among us" (John 1:14). We are to incarnate the Word of God. We are to have our lives transformed by it, and our minds renewed by it.

Fourth, *we often hear the Word and then don't do it.* The will of God is thwarted by educating people beyond their obedience. Jesus taught: "If you know these things, you are blessed if you do them" (John 13:17).

Fifth, *like the Pharisees, we tend to neglect the commandment of God and hold to the traditions of men* (Mark 7:8). I believe this is one of the most serious problems affecting our churches today. Many seminary graduates are called as "new wine" (zealous to serve God according to the truth of His Word) to "old wineskin" churches (rooted in the traditions of men), and the results are disastrous for both.

Contentment in Light of Heaven

Do not lay up for yourselves treasures on earth, where moth
and rust destroy and where thieves break in and steal, but
lay up for yourselves treasures in heaven, where neither moth
nor rust destroys and where thieves do not break in and steal.
For where your treasure is, there your heart will be also.
Matthew 6:19-21 esv

Treasures on earth have two characteristics. First, according to the law of entropy, all systems become increasingly disorderly and eventually decay. Therefore, constant concern is necessary to maintain earthly treasures. Second, there will always be thieves who covet what others have. Therefore, security for our possessions is another concern.

After Jesus spoke about our possessions, He addressed our needs: "Do not be anxious about your life, what you will eat or what you will drink, nor about your body, what you will put on. Is not life more than food, and the body more than clothing?" (verse 25 esv). The King James Version translation of Matthew 6:25 says "take no thought for your life," emphasizing the mind as the seat of anxious thinking. Jesus asks, "Which of you by being anxious can add a single hour to his span of life?" (verse 27 esv). Anxiety will likely shorten our life span.

It's hard to be anxiety-free if we're worrying about needs and our possessions (even though we can't take them with us when we die). Storing up treasures in heaven is profitable both for this age and for the age to come. Peaceful existence and a sense of security come from meaningful relationships, not material possessions. Using people to gain possessions reveals what we treasure in our hearts. Peacemakers use their possessions to love people.

"Godliness with contentment is great gain, for we brought nothing into the world, and we cannot take anything out of the world. But if we have food and clothing, with these we will be content" (1 Timothy 6:6-8 esv). If we can't find contentment in ourselves, it's futile to look for it elsewhere. Paul said, "I have learned in whatever situation I am to be content" (Philippians 4:11 esv).

The Significant Dominion

Let Us make man in Our image, according to Our likeness;
and let them rule over the fish of the sea and over the birds
of the sky and over the cattle and over all the earth, and
over every creeping thing that creeps on the earth.
GENESIS 1:26

In the original creation, Adam didn't search for significance; he was significant. He was given rule over all the other creatures God created (Genesis 1:26-27). God created Adam and gave him a divine purpose for being here: to rule over all His creatures. Was Satan on the scene at creation? Yes. Was he the god of this world at that time? Not at all. Who had the dominion in the garden? Under the authority of God, Adam did, that is until Satan usurped his dominion when Adam and Eve fell. That's when Satan became the god of this world.

Do you realize that the significant dominion Adam exercised before the Fall has been restored to you as a Christian? That's part of your inheritance in Christ. Satan has no authority over you, even though he will try to deceive you into believing that he has. Because of your position in Christ, you have authority over him. You are seated with Christ in the heavenlies (Ephesians 2:6).

First John 3:8 says, "The Son of God appeared for this purpose, that He might destroy the works of the devil." The whole plan of God is to restore fallen humanity and establish the kingdom of God where Satan now reigns. This work of God is not just for our personal victory but for all of creation. "For the anxious longing of the creation waits eagerly for the revealing of the sons of God. For the creation was subjected to futility, not of its own will, but because of Him who subjected it, in hope that the creation itself will also be set free from its slavery to corruption into the freedom of the glory of the children of God" (Romans 8:19-21).

Three Principles of Success

Only be strong and very courageous, being careful to do according to all
the law that Moses my servant commanded you. Do not turn from it to the
right hand or to the left, that you may have good success wherever you go.
JOSHUA 1:7 ESV

Joshua's success didn't depend on favorable circumstances in the Promised Land nor on the cooperation of the Philistines. The Israelites would be successful and prosperous if they understood and believed God's Word and lived accordingly (Joshua 1:8). Remember, we can be successful in the eyes of the world and a complete failure in the eyes of God and vice versa. The first principle of success is to know God and His ways. "Let not the wise man boast in his wisdom, let not the mighty man boast in his might, let not the rich man boast in his riches, but let him who boasts boast in this, that he understands and knows me" (Jeremiah 9:23-24 ESV).

The second principle of success is to become the people God created us to be, which is God's will for our lives. Though Adam and Eve were created in the image and likeness of God (Genesis 1:26), their sin marred that image. For this reason, Paul admonishes us "to put on the new self, created after the likeness of God in true righteousness and holiness" (Ephesians 4:24 ESV). Sanctification is the process of becoming like God in righteousness and holiness. "This is the will of God, your sanctification" (1 Thessalonians 4:3 ESV). Scripture stresses character before career, maturity before ministry, and being before doing.

The third principle of success is to be a good steward of the time, talent, gifts, and treasures God has entrusted to us. "We are his workmanship, created in Christ Jesus for good works" (Ephesians 2:10 ESV). Only we can keep us from being successful.

The Full Armor of God

Therefore, take up the full armor of God, that you may be able to
resist in the evil day, and having done everything, to stand firm.
EPHESIANS 6:13

A primary element in our protection from Satan and evil is the armor that God has provided for us and instructed us to put on in Ephesians 6:13-17. When we put on the armor of God we are really putting on Christ (Romans 13:12-14). And when we put on Christ we take ourselves out of the realm of the flesh, where we are vulnerable to attack, and we place ourselves within the dominion of Christ, where the evil one cannot touch us. Satan has nothing in Christ (John 14:30), and to the extent that we put on Christ, the evil one cannot touch us (1 John 5:18). He can only touch that which is on his own level. That's why we are commanded, "Make no provision for the flesh" (Romans 13:14), meaning, "Don't live on Satan's level."

It would appear from the verb tenses in Ephesians 6:14-15 that three of the pieces of armor—belt, breastplate, and shoes—are already on you: "having girded…"; "having put on…"; "having shod…." These pieces of armor represent the elements of your protection made possible when you receive Jesus Christ and in which you are commanded to stand firm. The Greek tense of *having* signifies that the action it refers to was completed before we were commanded to stand firm. That's the logical way a soldier would prepare for action: He would put on his belt, breastplate, and shoes before attempting to stand firm. Likewise, we are to put on the full armor of God after having already put on Christ.

When you read through Ephesians 6:10-20, you will notice the emphasis on the active part we must play on behalf of our own spiritual defense: "be strong" (verse 10); "put on" and "stand firm" (verse 11); "take up," "be able," "resist," and "stand firm" (verse 13); "stand firm" (verse 14); "taking up" (verse 16); "take" (verse 17); "pray at all times" and "be on the alert" (verse 18).

Over the next several devotions we will consider each of the six pieces of armor from Ephesians 6:13-17.

The Belt of Truth

Having girded your loins with truth.

EPHESIANS 6:14

The first piece of armor for the Christian warrior is the belt of truth. Jesus said, "I am...the truth" (John 14:6). And because Christ is in you, the truth is in you. However, continuing to choose truth is not always easy. Since Satan's primary weapon is the lie, your belt of truth (which holds the other pieces of body armor in place) is continually being attacked. If he can disable you in the area of truth, you become an easy target for his other attacks.

You stand firm in the truth by relating everything you do to the truth of God's Word. If a thought comes to mind which is not in harmony with God's truth, dismiss it. If an opportunity comes along to say or do something which compromises or conflicts with truth, avoid it. Adopt a simple rule of behavior: If it's the truth, I'm in; if it's not the truth, count me out.

When you learn to live in the truth on a daily basis, you will grow to love the truth because you have nothing to hide. You never have to cover up to God or anyone else; everything you do is in the light. Furthermore, when you live in the truth you dislodge the lies of Satan, the father of lies (John 8:44). Remember that if Satan can deceive you into believing a lie, he can control your life.

Jesus prayed, "I do not ask You to take them out of the world, but to keep them from the evil one" (John 17:15). How? "Sanctify them in the truth; Your word is truth" (verse 17). You will only dislodge Satan's lies in the light of God's revelation, and not by human reasoning or research.

The only thing a Christian ever has to admit to is the truth. Walking in the light and speaking the truth in love may seem threatening to some. But in reality, truth is a liberating friend and the only path to fellowship with God.

The Breastplate of Righteousness

Having put on the breastplate of righteousness.

EPHESIANS 6:14

The second piece of armor God has provided for us is the breastplate of righteousness. When you put on Christ at salvation you are justified before our holy God. It's not your righteousness but Christ's (1 Corinthians 1:30; Philippians 3:8-9). So when Satan aims an arrow at you by saying, "You're not good enough to be a Christian," you can respond with Paul, "Who will bring a charge against God's elect? God is the one who justifies" (Romans 8:33). Your righteousness in Christ is your protection against Satan's accusations.

Even though we rejoice in our position of righteousness in Christ, we are well aware of our deeds of unrighteousness when we think, say, or do something apart from God. Standing firm in our righteousness requires us to live in continuous agreement with God according to 1 John 1:9: "If we confess our sins, He is faithful and righteous to forgive us our sins and to cleanse us from all unrighteousness." Confession is different from saying "I'm sorry" or asking forgiveness. To confess (*homologeo*) means to acknowledge or to agree. You confess your sin when you say what God says about it: "I entertained a lustful thought, and that's a sin"; "I treated my spouse unkindly this morning, and that was wrong"; "Pride motivated me to seek that board position, and pride doesn't belong in my life."

Satan will make confession as difficult for you as he can. He will try to convince you that it's too late for confession, that God has already erased your name out of the book of life. That's another one of his lies. You're in Christ; you're already forgiven. You are the righteousness of God in Christ (2 Corinthians 5:21), and He will never leave you. Your relationship with God and your eternal destiny are not at stake when you sin, but your daily victory is. Your confession of sin clears the way for the fruitful expression of righteousness in your daily life. We should be like Paul, who said, "I also do my best to maintain always a blameless conscience both before God and before men" (Acts 24:16).

The Shoes of Peace

Having shod your feet with the preparation of the gospel of peace.

EPHESIANS 6:15

The next piece of armor is the shoes of peace. When you receive Christ you are united with the Prince of Peace. You have peace with God right now (Romans 5:1), but the peace of Christ must also rule in your heart if you are going to live victoriously, and that is possible only when you let the Word of Christ richly dwell in you (Colossians 3:15-16).

The shoes of peace become protection against the divisive schemes of the devil when you act as a peacemaker among believers (Romans 14:19). Peacemakers bring people together by promoting fellowship and reconciliation. "Blessed are the peacemakers, for they shall be called sons of God" (Matthew 5:9). Anyone can divide a fellowship, but it takes the grace of God to unite us in Him.

Too many Christians insist on common doctrine as the basis for fellowship. They reason that if we don't think the same and believe the same, there is no basis for peace. But common doctrine isn't the basis for fellowship; common heritage is. We're all children of God. If you wait to fellowship with someone until you agree perfectly on every point of doctrine, you'll be the loneliest Christian on earth. Instead of insisting on the unity of the mind, preserve the unity of the Spirit by taking the initiative to be the peacemaker in your relationships (Ephesians 4:3).

Some people like to play the devil's advocate in their relationships and churches. I ask, *Why?* He doesn't need any help! In His high priestly prayer, Jesus prayed, "I in them and you in me, that they may become perfectly one, so that the world may know that you sent me" (John 17:23 ESV). We have the promise that "the God of peace will soon crush Satan under your feet" (Romans 16:20). Ask God to use you to bring unity to your relationships by making you a peacemaker.

The Shield of Faith

*Taking up the shield of faith with which you will be able
to extinguish all the flaming missiles of the evil one.*

EPHESIANS 6:16

Paul mentions three more pieces of armor that we must take up to
protect ourselves from Satan's attack: the shield of faith, the helmet
of salvation, and the sword of the Spirit, which is the Word of God. The
first three (the belt of truth, the breastplate of righteousness, the shoes
of peace) are established by our position in Christ; these last three help
us continue to win the battle.

Contrary to popular perception, there is nothing mystical about
faith. Biblical faith is simply what you believe about God and His Word.
The more you know about God and His Word, the more faith you will
have. The less you know, the smaller your shield will be and the easier it
will be for one of Satan's fiery darts to reach its target. If you want your
shield of faith to grow large and protective, your knowledge of God and
His Word must increase (Romans 10:17).

These flaming missiles from Satan are nothing more than smoldering
lies, burning accusations, and fiery temptations bombarding our minds.
When a deceptive thought, accusation, or temptation enters your mind,
meet it head-on with what you know to be true about God and His Word.
How did Jesus deflect the missiles of Satan's temptation? By shielding
Himself with statements from the Word of God. Every time you memorize a Bible verse, listen to a sermon, or participate in a Bible study,
you increase your knowledge of God and enlarge your shield of faith.

We all struggle with tempting and accusing thoughts. If you are a
healthy and mature Christian, they will bounce right off your shield of
faith.

The Helmet of Salvation

And take the helmet of salvation.

The next necessary piece of spiritual armor is the helmet of salvation. Should your shield of faith be a little leaky and your daily victory elusive, be confident that the helmet of salvation guarantees your eternal victory. In the metaphor of armor, the helmet also secures coverage for the most critical part of your anatomy: your mind, where spiritual battles are either won or lost. As you struggle with the world, the flesh, and the devil on a daily basis, stand firm knowing that your salvation does not come and go with your success or failure in spiritual battle; your salvation is your eternal possession. You are a child of God, and nothing can separate you from the love of Christ (Romans 8:35).

People experiencing spiritual conflict tend to question their salvation or doubt their identity in Christ. Satan may disrupt your daily victory, but he can do nothing to disrupt your position in Christ. However, if he can get you to believe that you are not in Christ, you will live as though you are not, even though you are secure in Him.

The Christian warrior wears the helmet of salvation in the sense that he is the receiver and possessor of deliverance, clothed and armed in the victory of his Head, Jesus Christ. Satan is the ruler of this world, and the whole world is in his power (John 12:31; 1 John 5:19). Therefore, we are still in his territory as long as we are present in our physical bodies. But since we are joined to the Lord Jesus Christ, the devil has no legitimate claim on us, for Christ has "delivered us from the domain of darkness, and transferred us to the kingdom of His beloved Son" (Colossians 1:13). The helmet of our position in Christ assures us of ultimate victory over Satan.

The Sword of the Spirit

And take...the sword of the Spirit, which is the word of God.
EPHESIANS 6:17

The Word of God is the only offensive weapon mentioned in the list of armor. Since Paul used *rhema* instead of *logos* for "word" in Ephesians 6:17, I believe Paul is referring to the spoken Word of God. We are to defend ourselves against the evil one by speaking aloud God's Word.

Why is it so important to speak God's Word in addition to believing it and thinking it? Because Satan is a created being, and he doesn't perfectly know what you're thinking. By observing you, he can pretty well tell what you are thinking, just as any student of human behavior can. And it isn't difficult for him to know what you're thinking if he put the thought in. But he doesn't know what you're going to do before you do it. He can put thoughts into your mind, and he will know whether you buy his lie by how you behave.

Satan can try to influence you by planting thoughts in your head, but he can't read your thoughts. If you're going to resist Satan, you must do so verbally so he can understand you and be put to flight.

You can communicate with God in your mind and spirit because He knows the thoughts and intents of your heart (Hebrews 4:12). Your unspoken communion with God is your private sanctuary; Satan cannot eavesdrop on you. But by the same token, if you only tell Satan with your thoughts to leave, he won't leave because he is under no obligation to obey your thoughts. *You must defeat Satan by speaking out.* The good news is that most direct attacks occur at night or when you are alone.

One night I woke up absolutely terrified for no apparent reason, and I knew it was an attack from Satan. Without lifting my head from the pillow, I applied the two-step remedy suggested in James 4:7. In the sanctuary of my heart, I submitted to God. Then I was able to resist Satan with one spoken word—Jesus—and the fear was instantly and totally gone. I went back to sleep in complete peace.

The Expression of Pride

Pride goes before destruction, and a haughty spirit before stumbling.
PROVERBS 16:18

Pride is a killer. Pride says, "I can do it alone. I can get myself out of this mess without God's help." Oh, no you can't! We absolutely need God, and we desperately need each other. Paul wrote, "We are the true circumcision, who worship in the Spirit of God and glory in Christ Jesus and put no confidence in the flesh" (Philippians 3:3). Humility is confidence properly placed. Examine the instructions on pride and humility in James 4:6-10 and 1 Peter 5:1-10. The context reveals that spiritual conflict follows the expression of pride. Pride is what caused Lucifer to be thrown out of heaven.

Jesus said, "Simon, Simon [Peter], behold, Satan has demanded permission to sift you like wheat" (Luke 22:31). On what basis could Satan make that demand? The context reveals the answer: "There arose also a dispute among them as to which one of them was regarded to be greatest" (Luke 22:24). Pride was Peter's downfall, and it opened the door to the devil's opposition.

The Lord says that pride goes before destruction and an arrogant spirit before stumbling (Proverbs 16:18). We must confess areas where we have not denied ourselves, picked up our cross daily, and followed Him (Matthew 16:24). In so doing we have given ground to the enemy in our lives.

Have we believed that we could be successful and live victoriously by our own strength and resources? We must confess that we have sinned against God by placing our will before His and by centering our lives around self instead of Him. We must renounce the self life and by so doing cancel all the ground that has been gained in our members by the enemies of the Lord Jesus Christ.

The humble servant will do nothing from selfishness or empty conceit, and with humility of mind we will regard others as more important than ourselves (Philippians 2:3). A true disciple will serve others and in honor prefer others (Romans 12:10).

A Matter of Being Someone

If any man is in Christ, he is a new creature; the old
things passed away; behold, new things have come.

2 Corinthians 5:17

Being a Christian is not just a matter of getting something; it's a matter of being someone. A Christian is not simply a person who gets forgiveness, who gets to go to heaven, who gets the Holy Spirit, who gets a new nature. A Christian, in terms of our deepest identity, is a saint, a spiritually born child of God, a divine masterpiece, a child of light, a citizen of heaven. Being born again transformed you into someone who didn't exist before. What you receive as a Christian isn't the point; it's who you are. It's not what you do as a Christian that determines who you are; it's who you are that determines what you do (2 Corinthians 5:17; Ephesians 2:10; 1 Peter 2:9-10; 1 John 3:1-2).

Understanding your identity in Christ is absolutely essential to your success at living the Christian life. No person can consistently behave in a way that's inconsistent with the way he perceives himself. If you think you're of no good, you'll probably live like you are of no good. But if you see yourself as a child of God who is spiritually alive in Christ, you'll begin to live in victory and freedom as He lived. Next to a knowledge of God, a knowledge of who you are is by far the most important truth you can possess.

After years of working with people who are in deep spiritual conflict, I found one common denominator: None of them knew who they were in Christ. None knew of their spiritual heritage. All questioned their salvation and the love of God. Are you aware that there is someone alive and active in the world today who is dead set against you seeing yourself as spiritually alive and complete in Christ? Satan can do nothing to damage your position in Christ. But if he can deceive you into believing his lie—that you are not acceptable to God and that you'll never amount to anything as a Christian—then you will live as if you have no position or identity in Christ.

Our Most Important Assignment

If anyone does not provide for his own, and especially for those of his household, he has denied the faith, and is worse than an unbeliever.
1 TIMOTHY 5:8

When *love* is used as a verb in the Bible it requires the lover to meet the needs of the one being loved. Love must be given away. God so loved the world that He *gave* (John 3:16). The corollary to John 3:16 is 1 John 3:16-18: "We know love by this, that He laid down His life for us; and we ought to lay down our lives for the brethren…Let us not love with word or with tongue, but in deed and truth."

The essence of love is meeting needs, and our most important assignment from God is to meet the needs of those who are closest to us (1 Timothy 5:8). We tend to use the people closest to us instead of meeting their needs. So the busy homemaker is out resolving everybody else's child-rearing problems but her own. The pastor is available to everyone but his wife and children. And the executive will work overtime to solve company problems while ignoring needs at home.

Take an inventory of your family's needs. I'm not talking about the external needs like clothing, education, and food. I'm talking about gut-level needs that determine their sense of worth and belonging. When was the last time you hugged your child and told him you loved him? Have you noticed good character qualities in your spouse and pointed them out? If all you ever point out is physical qualities or achievements, your family members will base their worth on how well they perform and look instead of developing character. Do you regularly reinforce good behavior, or do you only notice the poor behavior? When your child does something nice, do you thank him? Does your child know that he is loved and valued from the way you talk to him?

Love can't be separated from action. Jesus said, "If you love Me, you will keep My commandments" (John 14:15). If you love your family members, follow through with loving words and deeds.

The Great Eternal Constant

*See how great a love the Father has bestowed upon
us, that we should be called children of God.*

1 John 3:1

Have you ever felt that God is ready to give up on you because, instead of walking confidently in faith, you sometimes stumble and fall? Do you ever fear that there is a limit to God's tolerance for your failure and that you are walking dangerously near that outer barrier or have already crossed it? I have met a lot of Christians like that. They think that God is upset with them, that He is ready to dump them, or that He has already given up on them because their daily performance is less than perfect.

It's true that the walk of faith can sometimes be interrupted by moments of personal unbelief or rebellion, or even satanic deception. It's during those moments when we think that God has surely lost His patience with us and is ready to give up on us. The temptation is to give up, stop walking by faith altogether, slump dejectedly by the side of the road, and wonder, *What's the use?* We feel defeated, God's work for us is suspended, and Satan is elated.

The primary truth you need to know about God in order for your faith to remain strong is that His love and acceptance is unconditional. When your walk of faith is strong, God loves you. When your walk of faith is weak, God loves you. When you're strong one moment and weak the next, strong one day and weak the next, God loves you. God's love for you is the great eternal constant in the midst of all the inconsistencies of your daily walk.

God wants us to do good, of course. The apostle John wrote: "I write this to you so that you will not sin" (1 John 2:1 NIV). But John continued by reminding us that God has already made provision for our failure so His love continues constant in spite of what we do: "But if anybody does sin, we have one who speaks to the Father in our defense—Jesus Christ, the Righteous One. He is the atoning sacrifice for our sins, and not only for ours but also for the sins of the whole world" (verses 1-2 NIV).

Furthest from God

When all the people saw the thunder and the flashes of lightning and the sound of the trumpet and the mountain smoking, the people were afraid and trembled, and they stood far off and said to Moses, "You speak to us, and we will listen; but do not let God speak to us, lest we die."
Exodus 20:18-19 ESV

The people of God were encamped at the base of Mount Sinai when "Moses went up to God" (Exodus 19:3). On the third day, the Lord was going to come down on the mountain, but the people were not to go up or they would die. Nobody present that day denied the existence of God.

Two characteristics define those who are furthest from God. First, those who stand "far off" prefer a secondhand relationship with God. They are content to let their pastor or priest study and pray for them. Second, their orientation toward God is to avoid punishment. They live as though the hammer of God could fall on them for the slightest mistake.

But the hammer already fell! It fell on Christ! We are not sinners in the hands of an angry God; we are saints in the hands of a loving God. "Since we have confidence to enter the holy places by the blood of Jesus…let us draw near with a true heart in full assurance of faith, with our hearts sprinkled clean from an evil conscience" (Hebrews 10:19-22 ESV).

Second Furthest from God

Then Moses and Aaron, Nadab, and Abihu, and seventy of the
elders of Israel went up, and they saw the God of Israel. There was
under his feet as it were a pavement of sapphire stone, like the very
heaven for clearness. And he did not lay his hand on the chief men
of the people of Israel; they beheld God, and ate and drank.
Exodus 24:9-11 ESV

The barrier to the mountain was a test for the Israelites to instill the fear of God to keep them from sinning (Exodus 20:20). The numbers drop off sharply when climbing the mountain of God. These 74 people had an unmistakable encounter with God, but when they were asked to wait until Moses returned, they grew impatient, went back down the mountain, and built a golden calf.

Mountain-top experiences can be exhilarating, but they don't last. We don't build golden calves when we backslide, but we create other gods like appearance, performance, social status, career, family, and temporal gratifications. "Is there a God?" is not the question lukewarm Christians are asking. They're asking, "So what? I believe in God, and I will pay homage to Him, but I have to get on with my [natural] life."

Jesus is our life, and knowing Him defines how we live now and for all eternity. When we love Jesus and others as ourselves, we are living as God originally intended. Godliness is profitable for this age and the age to come.

Second Closest to God

*The Lord said to Moses, "Come up to me on the mountain and wait
there, that I may give you the tablets of stone, with the law and the
commandment, which I have written for their instruction." So Moses rose
with his assistant Joshua, and Moses went up into the mountain of God.*
Exodus 24:12-13 ESV

Now only two are climbing the mountain of God, but why Joshua?
Moses pitched a tent outside the camp and called it "the tent
of meeting" (Exodus 33:7 ESV). When Moses went into the tent to
meet with God, the people would stand outside their tents and worship. "When Moses turned again into camp, his assistant Joshua the
son of Nun, a young man, would not depart from the tent" (verse 11).
Joshua was like Elisha, who would not depart when Elijah told him to
stay while he went on.

Some people aren't satisfied fulfilling religious obligations. Instead,
they see what Moses and Elijah had and want it for themselves. They
are like Paul, who said,

> Not that I have already obtained this or am already per-
> fect, but I press on to make it my own, because Christ
> Jesus has made me his own. Brothers, I do not consider
> that I have made it my own. But one thing I do: forgetting
> what lies behind and straining forward to what lies ahead,
> I press on toward the goal for the prize of the upward call
> of God in Christ Jesus (Philippians 3:12-14 ESV).

Closest to God

Thus the LORD used to speak to Moses face to
face, as a man speaks to his friend.
Exodus 33:11 ESV

Moses had a unique calling, and he had four qualifiers that made intimacy with God a reality. We can emulate those qualities.

First, Moses was humble, more than others (Numbers 12:3). Second, he was free from selfish ambition (Exodus 32:9-12), refusing God's offer to make a great nation of him because he was more concerned about God's reputation. Third, his goal in life was to know God and His ways (33:13). Fourth, he desired to see God's glory (verse 18).

In the Gospels, a multitude of people came to hear and be healed, but then they went back home. Of the Twelve, three climbed the mountain and saw the Lord transfigured along with Moses and Elijah. Of the three, "there was reclining on Jesus' bosom one of His disciples, whom Jesus loved" (John 13:23 NASB1995). Only one stayed with Jesus all the way to the cross. It was to John that Jesus said, "Behold, your mother!" (19:27 ESV). The two closest people to God at that time were linked together for the duration of their years.

A vacant place remains on the bosom of Jesus, waiting for anyone who believes that an intimate relationship with God is the ultimate pursuit of life.

Abiding in Christ

*I am the true vine, and my Father is the vinedresser. Every branch
in me that does not bear fruit he takes away, and every branch
that does bear fruit he prunes, that it may bear more fruit.*
JOHN 15:1-2 ESV

Fruit is the evidence of life, but the fruit doesn't grow off the vine.
The fruit grows off the ends of the branches that are organically con-
nected to the vine. Vineyards are pruned every year so they will bear
more fruit. The dead branches are cut off so they won't interfere with the
living branches, which are trimmed back. If branches are not trimmed,
they will grow like a bush and the leaves will crowd out the fruit. This is
not a hacking process. God knows how and when to trim each branch
so as not to damage it. If the branch splits, it dies.

That is why we should not play the role of God in another person's
life. "He will convict the world concerning sin and righteousness and
judgment" (John 16:8 ESV). When God convicts someone of sin, they
feel remorseful, and with that conviction comes the power to change.
When we attempt to convict others of sin, they become defensive, and
that bears no fruit.

That doesn't mean we shouldn't correct someone caught in sin or discipline them, but the emphasis should be on correction, not condemnation. In all cases, allow God to be the one who brings conviction for the
sin. Our job is to confront the sin and, in some cases, determine proper
consequences—but not to hammer them home. Graceful correction
brings about "the peaceful fruit of righteousness" (Hebrews 12:11 ESV).

Bearing Fruit

Abide in me, and I in you. As the branch cannot bear fruit by itself, unless it abides in the vine, neither can you, unless you abide in me. I am the vine; you are the branches. Whoever abides in me and I in him, he it is that bears much fruit, for apart from me you can do nothing…By this my Father is glorified, that you bear much fruit and so prove to be my disciples.
JOHN 15:4-5, 8 ESV

The pressure is on us! We have to bear fruit, right? No, we don't! We have to abide in Christ, because if we abide in Christ, then we will bear fruit. The fruit is just the evidence that we are abiding in Christ. Apart from Christ we can do nothing of eternal significance. The work we accomplish independently of God is wood, hay, and straw, which will burn up when tested by fire in the final judgment (1 Corinthians 3:11 and following).

Jesus said, "By this all people will know that you are my disciples, if you have love for one another" (John 13:35 ESV), which might appear to be even more pressure to perform. Now we have to do our best to love one another. No, we don't! Loving one another is the evidence that we have become disciples of Christ. The life of Christ flows through those disciples who abide in Him. We glorify God by manifesting His presence in our lives.

It does come with challenges. The more fruit we bear, the more criticism we invite. "Indeed, all who desire to live a godly life in Christ Jesus will be persecuted" (2 Timothy 3:12 ESV). But it will all be worth it. Nothing is more fulfilling than to be an instrument in God's hand and to participate with Him in healing wounds and setting captives free. To rescue the perishing, we must weather the storm.

Pruning the Branches

Every branch that bears fruit, He prunes it, that it may bear more fruit.
JOHN 15:2

Our goal is to abide in Christ, not to bear fruit. Jesus promised that if we abide in Him, we will bear much fruit (John 15:5).

In order that we may bear more fruit, God the Father prunes us. Sometimes well-meaning Christians have cut too much too soon, hindering growth. A dear but sadly abused child of God pictured her experience in the following poem:

> A friend of mine whose grapevine died, had put it out for trash.
>
> I said to her, "I'll take that vine and make something of that."
>
> At home the bag of dead, dry vines looked nothing but a mess.
>
> But as I gently bent one vine, entwining round and round, a rustic wreath began to form, potential did abound.
>
> One vine would not go where it should, and anxious as I was, I forced it so to change its shape, it broke—and what the cause?
>
> If I had taken precious time to slowly change its form, it would have made a lovely wreath, not a dead vine, broken, torn.
>
> As I finished bending, adding blooms, applying trim, I realized how that rustic wreath is like my life within.
>
> You see, so many in my life have tried to make me change. They've forced my spirit anxiously, I tried to rearrange.
>
> But when the pain was far too great, they forced my fragile form;
>
> I plunged far deeper in despair, my spirit broken, torn.

Then God allowed a gentle one who knew of dying vines, to kindly, patiently allow the Lord to take His time.

And though the vine has not yet formed a decorative wreath, I know that with God's servant's help one day when Christ I meet.

He'll see a finished circle, a perfect gift to Him.

It will be a final product, a wreath with all the trim.

So as you look upon this gift, the vine round and complete, remember God is using you to gently shape His wreath.

Notes

1. Chrysostom, quoted in *Ancient Christian Commentary on Scripture: New Testament*, Vol. XI (James), Gerald Bray ed., Thomas C. Oden, gen. ed. (Downer's Grove, IL: IVP Academic, 2000), 39.
2. C.S. Lewis, *Screwtape Letters* (Old Tappan, NJ: Fleming H. Revell, 1978).

Can We Help You Make Fruitful Disciples?

FREEDOM IN CHRIST

The purpose of Freedom in Christ Ministries (FICM) is to equip the church worldwide, enabling them to establish their people, marriages, and ministries alive and free in Christ through genuine repentance and faith in God to His honor and glory. The goal is to make fruitful disciples who can reproduce themselves and make an impact in their community.

We have offices or representatives in over forty countries and some representation in many more: see www.freedominchrist.org. Our passion is to help church leaders develop a discipleship strategy that will be effective for years to come. Contact our International Office to learn how we can establish an office in your country, or equip an individual representative in your country.

How can we help your church?

We offer:

- Online training for Discipleship Counseling: see www.ficm .org and click on CFM University.
- Introductory Seminars
- Advice on establishing a discipleship strategy for your church
- Training and equipping for those who will be involved in implementing that strategy
- A discipleship course in many languages to be used in churches leading participants through a repentance process that establishes them alive and free in Christ
- Many other resources on marriage, depression, fear, anger, etc. See the following pages.

Freedom in Christ Ministries
Books and Resources

Core Material

Victory Over the Darkness has a companion study guide, and DVD, as well as an audiobook edition (Bethany House, 2000). With more than 1,400,000 copies in print, this core book explains who you are in Christ, how to walk by faith in the power of the Holy Spirit, how to be transformed by the renewing of your mind, how to experience emotional freedom, and how to relate to one another in Christ.

The Bondage Breaker has a companion study guide, and audiobook edition (Harvest House Publishers, 2000). With more than 1,400,000 copies in print, this book explains spiritual warfare, what our protection is, ways that we are vulnerable, and how we can live a liberated life in Christ.

Discipleship Counseling (Bethany House, 2003) combines the concepts of discipleship and counseling and teaches the practical integration of theology and psychology helping Christians resolve their personal and spiritual conflicts through genuine repentance and faith in God.

The Steps to Freedom in Christ and the companion interactive video (Bethany House, 2017) are discipleship counseling tools that help Christians resolve their personal and spiritual conflicts through genuine repentance and faith in God.

Restored is an expansion of the *The Steps to Freedom in Christ* with additional explanation and instruction. It can be freely downloaded at www.restored.pub.

Walking In Freedom (Bethany House, 2009) is a 21-day devotional to be used for follow-up after processing *The Steps to Freedom in Christ*.

Freedom in Christ (Bethany House, 2017) is a discipleship course for Sunday school classes and small groups. The course includes a leader's guide, a student guide, and a DVD covering 10 lessons and *The Steps to Freedom in Christ*. This course is designed to enable believers to resolve personal and spiritual conflicts and be established alive and free in Christ.

The Bondage Breaker DVD Experience (Harvest House, 2011) is also a discipleship course for Sunday school classes and small groups. It is similar to the one above, but the lessons are 15 minutes long instead of 30 minutes. It has a companion interactive workbook, but no leaders guide.

"Victory Series" (Bethany House, 2014–2015) is a comprehensive curriculum, including eight books that follow the growth sequence of being rooted in Christ, growing in Christ, living in Christ, and overcoming in Christ: *God's Story for You; Your New Identity; Your Foundation in Christ; Renewing Your Mind; Growing in Christ; Your Life in Christ; Your Authority in Christ; Your Ultimate Victory*.

Specialized Books

The Bondage Breaker, The Next Step (Harvest House, 2011) includes several testimonies of people who found their freedom from all kinds of problems, with commentary by Dr. Anderson. It is an important learning tool for encouragers, and gives hope to those who are entangled in sin.

Overcoming Addictive Behavior with Mike Quarles (Bethany House, 2003) explores the path to addiction and how a Christian can overcome addictive behaviors.

Overcoming Depression with Joanne Anderson (Bethany House, 2004) explores the nature of depression, which is a body, soul, and spirit problem and presents a wholistic answer for overcoming this "common cold" of mental illnesses.

Daily in Christ with Joanne Anderson (Harvest House, 2000) is a popular daily devotional read by thousands of internet subscribers every day.

Who I Am in Christ (Bethany House, 2001) has 36 short chapters describing who believers are in Christ and how their deepest needs are met in Him.

Freedom from Addiction with Mike and Julia Quarles (Bethany House, 1996) begins with Mike and Julia's journey into addiction and codependency, and explains the nature of chemical addictions and how to overcome them in Christ.

One Day at a Time with Mike and Julia Quarles (Bethany House, 2000) is a 120-day devotional helping those who struggle with addictive behaviors and explaining how to discover the grace of God on a daily basis.

Letting Go of Fears with Rich Miller (Harvest House Publishers, 2018) explains the nature of fear, anxiety and panic attacks and how to overcome them.

Setting Your Church Free with Charles Mylander (Bethany House, 2014) explains servant leadership and how the leadership of a church can resolve corporate conflicts through corporate repentance.

Setting Your Marriage Free with Charles Mylander (Bethany House, 2014) explains God's divine plan for marriage and the steps that couples can take to resolve their difficulties.

Christ-Centered Therapy with Terry and Julianne Zuehlke (Zondervan, 2000) explains the practical integration of theology and psychology for professional counselors, and provides them with biblical tools for therapy.

Managing Your Anger with Rich Miller (Harvest House, 2018) explains the nature of anger and how to put away all anger, wrath, and malice.

Grace That Breaks the Chains with Rich Miller and Paul Travis (Harvest House, 2014) explains the bondage of legalism and how to overcome it by the grace of God.

Winning the Battle Within (Harvest House, 2008) shares God's standards for sexual conduct, the path to sexual addiction, and how to overcome sexual strongholds.

Restoring Broken Relationships (Bethany House, 2015) explains the primary ministry of the church, and how we can be reconciled to God and each other.

Rough Road to Freedom (Monarch Books, 2012) is Dr. Anderson's memoir.

The Power of Presence (Monarch Books, 2016) is about experiencing the presence of God during difficult times and what our presence means to each other. This book is written in the context of Dr. Anderson caring for his wife, who is slowly dying with agitate dementia.

For more information or to purchase the above materials contact Freedom In Christ Ministries:

CANADA:
freedominchrist@sasktel.net
www.ficm.ca

UNITED KINGDOM:
info@ficm.org.uk
www.ficm.org.uk

UNITED STATES:
info@ficm.org
www.ficm.org

INTERNATIONAL:
www.freedominchrist.org